Ancient Moon Wisdom

The Kabbalistic Wheel of Astro Mystery and Its Relationship to the Human Experience

Miriam Maron

Hamilton Books

A member of
The Rowman & Littlefield Publishing Group
Lanham • Boulder • New York • Toronto • Plymouth, UK

Copyright © 2013 by Hamilton Books
4501 Forbes Boulevard, Suite 200, Lanham, Maryland 20706
Hamilton Books Aquisitions Department (301) 459-3366

10 Thornbury Road, Plymouth PL6 7PP, United Kingdom

Library of Congress Control Number: 2012946284
ISBN: 978-0-7618-5984-0 (paperback : alk. paper)—ISBN: 978-0-7618-5985-7 (electronic)

☉™ The paper used in this publication meets the minimum requirements of American National Standard for Information Sciences Permanence of Paper for Printed Library Materials, ANSI/NISO Z39.48-1992.

I dedicate this book to my father, Jacob Maron, זכר צדיק לברכה ("May the memory of the righteous bring us towards Blessing"), whose resourcefulness, intelligence, and strength helped him to not only survive the Holocaust, but also to bravely join the ranks of those committed to stopping Hitler's destruction. Eventually, although severely wounded in battle no less than eight times, he achieved the rank of colonel before marching into Berlin to participate in the climactic victory of the allies over a great human tragedy in world history. My father took his incredible strength, his amazing perseverance and foresight, and dedicated his life to the well-being and support of his family as well as others less fortunate. What he did for us and what he taught us is honored and appreciated beyond words and without end.

And

To my mother, Sonia Maron, שיחיה לאורך ימים טובים ארוכים ("May she live a lengthy life of immeasurable goodness"), whose love, tender-heartedness, endurance, empathy and support is forever memorable and deeply received within the hearts of those lucky enough to know her. She, too, survived the Holocaust, living for years on the run as a young teenager in daily dread and terror. She managed to transform her life's difficulties and has been a loving, hard-working, devoted mom, whom I will always be in awe of and will always treasure.

Contents

Preface

As a little girl growing up on a farm, I remember so vividly the gentle caress of the wind as I would run through the cornfields, and how the wind whispered to me about worlds beyond. It sang to me of distant realms whose passageways were welcoming of those who dared believe that there was more to life than life itself. My connection with Spirit, my awareness of forces and energies outside the known universe, fortified with every subsequent stroll across the land and with every phase of my personal maturation.

My youthful wonder at our amazing universe and the miracle of the human body eventually landed me at the University of Pennsylvania, where I completed a full pre-med as well as Nursing curriculum and worked as a Registered Nurse with a strong background in psychology (both in inpatient and outpatient settings). One day, later in my career, while working on a surgical unit as a Head Nurse, I observed a throat cancer patient smoking through his tracheostomy tube! This incident shocked me, and inspired me to further my academic studies in the field of Preventive Medicine. My passion, in other words, gradually became more about how to help people *not* get sick, and that is when I pursued my Masters in Exercise Physiology.

Throughout these phases of my work as an R.N. and a preventive medicine practitioner, I had this gnawing feeling deep down that there was more to the science of healing in *addition* to conventional medicine and holistic medicine. My background in Jewish studies, including Kabbalistic Meditation, as well as my lifelong attendance at "the University of Life Wisdom," alluded to yet another dimension that is often unattended: Soul Healing. Eventually, I was initiated as a Rabbi and years later earned my Doctorate in Kabbalistic Healing. My journey had taken me from the corridors of hospitals to the corridors of the human spirit, guiding clients in internal walks through portals of their soul-self least visited and which gifted them with a clarity for their life direction they had never thought possible. These inner journeys also brought to many a quality of psychological healing that had been unavailable to them through other venues. These venues included healing of old wounds and new ones, emotionally, psychically, and sometimes physically as well. More than guided meditation, these journeys involve truly hearing what the questions are and even more so hearing what lies *beneath* the questions. It has been of utmost importance in this work to see each situation independently and bring forth the appropriate tools most suitable for manifesting the best results.

The efficacy of these healing journeys are attributed to the mystical teachings around the birth time of the client combined with an open heart, many years of experience in intuitive listening, and a beautiful Divinely-Inspired connection that affords direction and support. As the Biblical Joseph said to the Pharaoh when he was asked to interpret the Pharaoh's disturbing dreams: "It is not within my power alone. Rather, the One Who Masters All Powers and Possibilities [*Elo'heem*] shall respond to the Pharaoh's quest for peace of mind" (Genesis 41:16).

In my many years of practice, I have enjoyed being visited by or "Skyping" with international clientele, some of whom were trained in a variety of paradigms, including many mainstream physicians and psychologists who requested personal explorations within this amazing mode of healing. All were amazed at the precision of my readings and how specific and relevant they were to their life story, past and present.

The concepts behind the modality of my practice is based primarily on a blend of many years of study and experience, psychological training, personal intuition, hands-on healing, and ancient Hebraic mystery wisdom. This wisdom, much of which is drawn from Hebrew and Judeo-Aramaic source texts, is comprised of rituals, incantations, and shamanic journeying while also gleaning the mystery wisdom handed down through the ages around the cycle of the months on the Hebraic calendar. I have had the pleasure of meeting with clients of different religious and cultural backgrounds and those with no particular association. I found that when I applied this wisdom along with other eclectic techniques to a client's situation, we would both walk away from the session awed and thoroughly amazed at the depth and accuracy with which this work would address the client's personal and specific circumstances, challenges and possible resolutions.

This wisdom is based on an ancient wheel of moons and their attributes found in some of the older Kabbalistic (Jewish mystical) writings, as well as the accompanying teachings related to those qualities. The more I studied this long-neglected body of wisdom, and the more I applied it in my private work with people, the more apparent it became to me that this knowledge would be helpful to anyone with a desire to learn more about their challenges and their gifts, and how to more easily work with both. And so, this book was born. It does not contain every detail of how this system works, which would take volumes, but communicates the essentials of these teachings in a way that I believe can benefit anyone, regardless of religious or cultural background.

This is a book that will familiarize readers with the gifts of each moon, its corresponding tribal quality, totem, stone, herb, Hebrew letter, and so on, so that readers can find themselves in their corresponding birth month and learn more about the nature of their Soul Journey™. This learning, in turn, will prove helpful in overcoming hurdles, in *understanding* hurdles, and in discovering clarity around those parts of our lives that appear to us otherwise quite muddled. I have written this book in such a way that regardless of one's birth month, one will find relevance in connecting with any of the monthly phases as they move through the yearly cycle.

Over the years I learned a great deal about the richness of my heritage and its history, the depth of its aboriginal wisdom, and the very eclectic tribal characteristics of my people. It is an honor and a privilege to share these ancient teachings and put them together in an easy-to-follow guide for all interested in the ageless wisdom of the sages and how they relate to our lives and our times. It is my hope that in sharing this with you, the reader, that you will be moved to explore the mysteries within as well as the deep Mystery of All that is shared in one way or another by *all* people.

I want to thank my children, Ryan Aaron and Sarina Aliya, for their patience during the lengthy process of bringing this book to its fruition. I will always be in appreciation of their willingness to forfeit time with me in order to allow for the birthing of this book, as well as time spent in sharing this wisdom with my students and clients.

I also want to acknowledge Rabbi Gershon Winkler for guiding me in locating some of the less accessible source texts and for helping with the editing phases of this book.

Finally, I want to thank Bogdan Knezevich for spending his time reviewing the manuscript and providing me with important editorial feedback.

Chapter One

The Moons

For in every single hour the universes shift, and one hour cannot be compared to another hour. And one who explores the matter of the journey of the constellations and stars, and the changes in their shifts and configurations, and how in a single moment they alter their situation whereby one who is born in that very moment is prone to circumstances that differ from one born into the moment just prior, will see and understand from this that the Upper Worlds are without end or number. [1]

The Hebraic tradition appears to hold contradictory teachings about the science of astrology. On the one hand, it asks us to abandon any consultation of the stars for clues to our destinies, and on the other hand there were great sages of Israel who would check their own horoscopes, let alone teach about the wisdom of the planetary configurations, days of the week, and so on. [2] There is also a teaching that anyone who has the capability of mastering this science and refrains from doing so, insults God, who creates it all. In fact, the teaching goes on, actively exploring the מזלות *mazalot*, or constellations is a sacred deed in itself. [3] Note how the Hebrew word for "constellations" is מזל *mazal*, which is why Jews the world over proclaim "Mazal Tov!" on momentous life-cycle occasions such as births and weddings. It is a two-word prayer expressing the hope that the astral configuration in that moment gifts the person or persons with blessings of all good. מזל *Mazal* means "astral arrangement," and טוב *Tov* means "good," or "as it ought to be." The study of the stars and the influences and lessons contained in their varying configurations was thus considered no less a way toward appreciation and consciousness of the Creator than the study of plants, wildlife and other phenomena of Earthly nature.

The fact is that Classical Judaism includes astrology as a legitimate study and science. The ancient teachers pushed for independent thinking and

choice making, and they therefore discouraged dependency upon forces outside of the gift of Free Will they held so dear. The study of astrology, while it
could not be discouraged, was rather tempered with the proverbial Jewish
"However" — as in, the sky beings have their influence, but you should not
become helplessly subject to them.[4] One might rather understand the astral
forces as predisposition, not as an absolute unbending cosmic decree. Free
Will, in other words, reigns supreme, reigns above and beyond the readings
one might get from the planets. On the other hand, such readings also prove
helpful in directing your life situation as you would direct a sail in relationship with the predisposition of the prevailing wind conditions during a sea
voyage. This wisdom, then, helps us to discover clues to the meaning behind
our challenges and how to work with them. Because, as with everything else
in life, Judaism teaches that astrology, too, is about being in relationship, a
relationship with the sky beings and what they might mirror back to you in
your daily life situation, and you to them.

    The most influential of the seven sky beings which the Hebrew tradition
considers most relative to our Earth walk (Mars, Sun, Moon, Jupiter, Saturn,
Mercury, Venus), is Moon, or ירח *ya'rey'ach,* literally "Traveler." Moon is
also referred to in Hebrew as לבנה *le'vanah,* feminine for "White" just as
Mars, for example, is called מאדים *m'adeem,* "Makes Red." The Hebraic
calendar is therefore lunar, and all the sacred festivals are determined by the
varying phases of the moon, which is why Jewish holidays never occur the
same time each year on the standard solar calendar. Accordingly, the Hebrew
word for "month" is חודש *cho'desh,* literally "renewal time," because in the
eyes of the human on Earth the moon is constantly renewing, never static,
never stuck. Every evening the moon appears differently, waxing and then
waning, growing and then shrinking, hidden and then visible, sometimes
only at night, sometimes also during the day. The moon is therefore considered a more powerful guide and influence for the ever dynamic life journey
and personal unfolding of the human. Every moment invites us toward
change or with the potential for change. Every day brings us up against
choices that shift our lives, and that have us waxing or waning, growing or
shrinking, hidden or seen.

    Reckoning time and influence by the moon is possibly one of several
remnants in the Hebrew tradition of ancient feminine spirituality. Unlike
conventional astrological science, which tends to reflect qualities of steadfast
principle and absolutes, lunar astrology is more reflective of the feminine
qualities of flexibility and process. The Sun, on the other hand, tends to be
more direct and linear, while the Moon tends to be more fluid and reflective.
Solar is more definitive, moon more process, more experiential.

    Of course, the Sun is not without its role in all this, it being, after all, the
very source of the light that is reflected by the moon. The moon, however, is
considered most immediately relevant to human personal life journeying.

The shifts we experience in our lives, like the lunar phases, are determined by reflections, by our orbit around people and circumstances and how we inflect and reflect those encounters. Or, for those on spiritual quests, the Sun can be seen as symbolic of the Creator, the Light of the Universe, and how we choose our orbit, our proximity, our inflection of the Great Light, is how we in turn *reflect* that light both to ourselves and to those who encounter us.

The initial sighting of that very thin sliver of the first moon phase is therefore a sacred event and celebration in Judaism. On the one hand, it may symbolize possession of very little God Light, or of being distant from the Creator, of being far from spiritual. On the other hand — the way the Hebrew tradition sees it — if someone is on the spiritual blink and they manage to open themselves up to so much as even a very thin sliver of the God Light, it is more dear to the Creator and more holy than someone who has already achieved full inflection of the Light. As the first-century Ben Hai-Hai put it: "Life's rewards are determined by one's efforts, not one's achievements."[5] The second-century sage Rabbi Yassa quotes the Creator as saying: "Open up for me but so much as the eye of a needle, and I in turn will open up for you passageways so wide that entire caravans of wagons and tents can pass through with the greatest of ease."[6] Or, as another sage quotes God as saying: "Take but one step toward me, and I shall meet you the rest of the way."[7]

Judaism understands the human process as an ever dynamic journey that is in constant motion in spite of our well-intentioned attempts at "settling down." No one is essentially all good or all bad, in other words, because we have choice, and can always change, for better or for worse. "Don't be so sure of yourself," taught the first-century B.C.E. sage, Hillel the Elder, "until the day of your death."[8] The phasing of the moon, therefore, symbolizes the human cyclic tendency to reach crescendos of enlightenment or inspiration or spiritual awareness, only to plummet into the abyss of confusion, alienation, or frustration. We all experience highs and lows, moments of faith and moments of doubt, moments of hope and moments of disappointment, moments of motivation and moments of being stuck. The lesson of the moon is that phases in themselves are natural and are part of our life process, and that the same forces which phase us into the darkness will in turn phase us gradually into the light, and that when we wane and drop and feel low and uninspired, this too is part of our growing, of our very aliveness. It is the exhale before the inhale. It is the predawn dimness before the daylight brightness, the chaos and emptiness which often precedes the emergence of renewal and creativity, just as it preceded the creation of the universe.[9]

Judaism therefore honors the gift of moon when it is with least light and when it is with most light. When it reflects its first light, it is celebrated as ראש חודש *rosh chodesh*, or "First [phase of] Renewal," while the seasonal festivals of the cycles of nature and of corresponding spiritual commemorations are celebrated when the moon is full. Both newness and fullness of the

moon, then, have their respective sacredness and celebration as does newness
and fullness in our lives. We must also remember that this sacredness is sown
in the seeming darkness that precedes newness in our lives. "One ought to
acknowledge Divine blessing in bad times," the ancient rabbis taught, "no
less than in good times."[10]

Basically, then, the ancient Hebrew twelve-month Zodiac mirrors the
twelve tribes of the ancient Hebrews, who descended from the twelve sons of
the patriarch Ya'akov יעקב (Jacob) and the matriarchs Ley'ah לאה, Ra'chel
רחל, Bil'hah בלהה and Zilpah זלפה.[11] The twelve sons are: Reuvayn ראובן,
Shim'on שמעון, Ley'vee לוי, Yehudah יהודה, Yee'sas'char יששכר, Zevulun
זבולון, Dahn דן, Naf'talee נפתלי, Gahd גד, Asher אשר, Yo'sef יוסף and
Bin'yamin בנימין. There was a thirteenth member of this founding family, the
sole *female* sibling: Deenah דינה. Applying the ancient midrashic technique
of creative interpretation, Deenah is keeper of the leap-year moon, Second
Adar, the additional thirteenth month added every several years to the Hebraic lunar calendar in order to keep up with the solar cycle.

Why the need to keep up with the solar cycle, when the Hebrew calendar
reckoning is based on the lunar cycle? Because, while the dance of Earth
around Sun has no bearing on the lunar calendar reckoning in itself, it is very
much relevant to determining the seasons of Summer and Winter, which, in
turn, affects the growth of the crops of grain. The pivotal point of the Hebraic
calendar reckoning is the Moon of Nee'sahn, the month in which the ancient
Hebrews were liberated from Egypt. This month, known in the Torah as
"First Month" for the Hebraic calendar reckoning, is also clearly pin-pointed
as the period of the renewal of the wheat crop, or in Hebrew: *cho'desh
ha'a'veev* חדש האביב,[12] which also translates as Moon of the Spring Season:
"For in the season of the renewal of the wheat crop [*Aveev*] did God take you
out of Egypt."[13] It is specifically *then* that the sacred rites of Passover are to
bc performed, and only on the fourteenth day of that month, when the moon
is at its fullest, and just before the moon begins to wane. And as First Month,
all the subsequent months are determined by its timing alone.

> The time for Passover is specifically called Renewal of *Aveev*, that it has to be
> a time of renewal. And *Aveev* is the cycle of Nee'sahn, for the "Nee'sahn" —
> the miraculous power — of the Sun enters into that time. For Nee'sahn is
> called "Aveev" due to it being the time of the ripening of the grain crop. And
> the ripening of the grain crop is dependent solely on the cycle of the Sun, as
> both Summer and Winter are determined by the cycle of the Sun. And the
> Torah specifically states about this season that we are to "guard the renewal of
> the season of the grain crop" (Deuteronomy 16:1), meaning that we are to
> make sure it falls within the season of renewal, and the term "renewal" applies
> only to the moon, for she is constantly involved in renewing herself, so to
> speak, in re-birthing her phases. And this is why the fourteenth day of the lunar
> cycle of Nee'sahn was designated for the Passover rites, because it is the

period during which the Sun renews our Earth and the phase of the moon is at the crescendo of *her* renewal since thereafter she begins to wane…. And thus you see how the fullness of the light of the moon during this period touches the fullness of the first light of the Sun that brings renewal to the Earth. So when it says "Guard the Moon of *Aveev*" it means make sure that the miraculous force of renewal of the Sun is drawn into the fullness of the renewal of the moon — that the moon completes its illumination along with the first ray of the Sun's renewal, and does not begin to darken before the arrival of the shining of the [first] Sun [of Spring].[14]

This drama of renewal in Nature is made possible by the position of the Earth in relation to the Sun during this period. Since the days of the lunar cycle — the phases of the moon — are a few days shorter than the days of the solar cycle, over time the lunar reckoning would slip significantly behind the solar cycle so that the celebration of the Passover and accompanying barley-offering rites, which needs to be during the period of renewal, of Spring, will end up occurring in Winter! Winter is neither a period of renewal nor of the coming to life of the grain crop. As the solar cycle is 365 days and the lunar yearly cycle is 354 days,[15] the lunar calendar reckoning would fall behind the solar reckoning by eleven days each year. Therefore, every several years, when the lunar cycle slip-slides back close to a month's worth of days, we add a second month to the last month preceding that of Nee'sahn, the month of Adar, in order to make sure that Passover always retains its solar connection in regards to being a period of renewal and to coincide with the beginnings of the grain crop. And we call this second moon simply Second Adar, or אדר שני *Adar Shay'nee*.

In ancient times, our people would not consider it a new moon time until the tribal elders declared it so, and the tribal elders would not declare the onset of the new moon until witnesses came to them or sent bonfire signals from distant hills indicating that someone had seen the first sliver of the moon.[16] The reason behind all this is the nature of our people's ways, which is very much rooted in flexibility, in leaving ample space for possibilities beyond fixed plans and definitions. To us, the world, life, the universe, is in constant flux, constant dance, and constant mystery, the wisdom of that mystery concealed and camouflaged within the obvious, waiting to be conjured and interpreted within the context of our personal life walk.

So even the teachings we have from our ancestors regarding what predisposition we each are born into, based on what phase of the moon, what day, what hour, what planetary influence, etc. — even these teachings are not meant to be etched in stone. They are not a one-size-fits-all set of standards. They are very individual, very personal, based on the ancient moon wisdom of our people and in conjunction with the particular life story of the individual. This wisdom is also helpful when used for monthly guidance as one moves through the calendar year. Each month holds a particular opening, or gate, for shift. Ancient Moon Wisdom is applicable for all, regardless of which month you were born into, and regardless of your religious or cultural affiliation or belief system.

Originally, we named our moons, or months, by their particular auspicious seasons of planting and harvesting. So the first month we'd call Moon of *Zee'v* זו,[17] "Radiance" (Spring). The second month we'd call Moon of Seeding Grapes, the third month Moon of planting Flax, fourth month First Cutting Harvest, fifth month, Moon of First Rains, sixth month Moon of Introspection, seventh month, Moon of the Ingathering in the Going Out of the Year[18] — which celebrates the Hebrew New Year and the harvest season at the beginning of Autumn. The seventh month was also known as the Moon of *Ey'tanim* איתנים, "Mighty Ones"[19] — referring to the ancestors Abraham, Isaac and Jacob, since it is believed that they were born in that month.[20] The eighth month was called the Moon of *Bool* בול, "Decay,"[21] since by then the fallen foliage of Autumn has decomposed.[22] The ninth, tenth and eleventh month were not named. They are basically Winter moons. No planting, no harvesting. The eleventh month is Moon of the New Year of the Trees,[23] as it is the time of the first flow of the sap, which continues into the twelfth month as Winter ebbs and introduces Spring.

When the ancient Hebrews returned to their ancestral homeland from their exile in Babylon approximately 2500 years ago, they adapted some of the names used in Mesopotamia and Hebraized them. So now we have Nee'sahn ניסן, Iyyar אייר, See'vahn סיון, Tamuz תמוז, Ahv אב, Elul אלול, Tish'ray תשרי, Chesh'von חשון, Kees'lev כסלו, Tey'vet טבת, Sh'vaht שבט and Adar אדר — known as the twelve months of the Hebraic calendar. But, again, since nothing is clear-cut and absolute in the lunar reckoning, we have that thirteenth month that arrives every several years to keep up with the cycle of the Sun. After all, with all the honor and ritual we encourage around the lunar phases, we do not neglect honoring the Sun as well, who provides the moon with her light. In fact, the second-century Rabbi Me'ir used to greet the Sun every dawn by running toward the blazing horizon with his arms outstretched in a gesture of welcome, and referred to the Sun as: "My brother!"[24] So in respect to the cycle of the Sun, we tack that thirteenth month onto our calendar every three years or so and label it *Second* Adar — *Adar Shay'nee* אדר שני.

Each month, along with its corresponding tribal archetype, highlights a quality that reflects a particular human attribute, such as anger, love, laughter, hearing, seeing, communicating, etc. Every month also has an Earthly attribute corresponding to the tribal Totem which the ancestors designated for each of the twelve tribal descendants of Jacob's children: seashore, water, canyon, lioness, wolf, snake, donkey, lion, oryx, buffalo, tree, antelope. Each month in turn has its light gift and its shadow cost, its positive characteristics and its negative inclinations, depending upon how responsibly or recklessly we manifest them in our daily lives. And, again, each month has its own quality reflective of the human characteristic most pronounced in the persona that unfolds during that particular month. These attributes stem from the stories surrounding the births as well as the characteristics of each child of Jacob as bestowed upon them first by Jacob and later by Moses. These stories provide us with further clarity as to the challenges and gifts of each moon.

Every one of the tribes had a particular gem stone assigned to them that was also sewn into the breastplate of the High Priest of Israel in ancient times,[25] as well as a species of plant or herb that was incorporated into the mysterious blend of the Sacred Incense ceremony, or קטורת *ke'to'ret*.[26] All of these symbols, whether represented in a particular month's tribal totem, tribal stone, or tribal plant, are helpful "handles" and imagery for deepening our absorption of the wisdom that each moon offers us. If you were born in the Moon of Adar, whose tribal totem is Wolf, you may want to study about the nature of Wolf and see how it relates to you and to your life. To help you feel more connected to the empowerment of your particular birth month you may want to carry the gemstone of that moon, or a small pouch with the herb of that moon, and so on. If you are a parent of a child who is "coming of age," such as a Bat- or Bar-Mitzvah, you may want to familiarize your child with their birth moon totems and incorporate the corresponding animal, stone, and plant of their birth moon into their ceremony. All of these earthy beings, whether stone, animal or plant, are not simply iconic in nature. They represent authentic portals of soul connection, as Judaism teaches about the interconnectivity of all beings. The souls of animals and humans, taught the thirteenth-century Rabbi Shlomo ben Aderet, are spirit relatives of one another.[27] In the more ancient Kabbalistic text of the Zohar, the most comprehensive compendium of ancient and early-medieval Jewish mysticism, we are taught that "the souls of animals and humans are imprinted upon each other."[28] Or, in the Biblical Book of Job:

> Ask the earth and she will tell you; speak to the animals and they will guide you. Inquire of the fishes of the sea and they will inform you.[29]

Every month in the Hebrew calendar also has a specific "House," its unique realm or arena where its attributes play themselves out. Each of these Houses is richly furnished with a distinct wisdom or quality created by the particular configuration or choreography of the seven sky beings during that month (Sun, Moon, Saturn, Mercury, Venus, Mars, and Jupiter). It is like re-arranging the furniture every month, so that from month to month the unique atmosphere of each rearrangement inspires something specific.

Everything in life, Judaism teaches, has its shadow side, its opposite realm. Accordingly, each month has its "Shadow Moon," situated directly opposite it on the ancient Hebrew Moon Wheel. Our Shadow Moon, we have to understand, is not there to taunt us or frustrate us. It is actually there to mirror back to us what we are lacking, what we may need to work on to help us move through the very obstacles it seems to set before us. The corresponding House of a Shadow Moon is therefore challenging and can stymie, but it can also be immensely beneficial to our life walk. It can help us overcome the forces that hold us back and inhibit us, or to redirect our flow.

The Jewish shamanic tradition correlates each of the monthly archetypes and their qualities to the mystery of a particular letter of the 22-lettered ancient Hebrew alphabet whose mystique is encrypted within its shape, in its numerical equivalent, and in its meaning. For example, the Hebraic letter ד *Da'let* means "Door" or "Passageway," and represents the number 4. ג *Gimmel* means "Camel," also "Doing," and represents the number 3. ט *Tet* is Snake and represents the number 9, and so on.

The significance of the letters in the Hebraic alphabet lies in the Jewish belief that God created the universe with these symbols. This is why the Hebrew word for "letter" is אות *o't*, which literally means Sign, or Symbol, and is often used to imply Miracle as well. In the ancient mystical sources, the letters of the Hebrew alphabet are referred to as אבנים *avanim*, or stones[30] since stones are keepers of memory,[31] in particular the memory of Genesis. Stones are also the building blocks of primal matter from which all of Creation emanated.[32] Each letter is considered a sacred vehicle for transmitting the intent of Creator for Creation to manifest. A very detailed mystical treatment of the Hebrew alphabet can be explored further in a book I co-authored, titled *Sacred Tongue*. Even for those who are not familiar with the Hebrew letters and its symbolism, they remain powerful tools of focus and inspiration, and are an added dimension and vibration to the quality and content provided in this book.

Finally, this wisdom also incorporates the Zodiacs, ancient tribal flags and colors corresponding to each of the months, as well as which of the directions each of the tribes were positioned during the forty-year desert journey from Egypt to Canaan.

Fundamentally, the secret of astrology is this: The universe emanates constantly from *ayn-sof* אין סוף — the "No End" (God) — who is always dynamic, never static. Thus, the universe is in constant motion and the arrangements of its planets and stars are constantly shifting. Therefore, when we are born, we are born into a whole new universe formed at that moment anew by the changes effected in the arrangements of the stars and planets that in turn have shifted in the hour of our birth because of the ever-dynamic dance of No End.

The teachings in this book are drawn from numerous ancient and early-medieval Aramaic and Hebraic source texts, including, but not limited to the following: The teachings regarding tribal totems, flags, colors, directions, as well as corresponding stones and herbs, are based on Genesis Chapter 49;

Exodus 28:17-21, 30:23 and 34-35; Deuteronomy, Chapter 33; *Midrash Ba-midbar Rabbah* 2:7; *Talmud Bav'li, Keree'tut* 6a. Further details such as houses of the months, zodiacs, correspondence of tribe to month, are based on the Ancient Hebrew Wheel of Astro Wisdom, which appears in the beginning of the second volume of *Sefer Etz Chayyim* by the 16th-century Kabbalist, Rabbi Chayyim Vital. An earlier version of this wheel appears in the commentary of the 12th-century Rabbi Avraham ibn Daud on the *Sefer Yetzirah*, folio 5a; also in *Ohr Hal'vanah*, folio 86. Numerous other ancient text references are provided in the endnotes of each chapter.

Customarily, the letter ו is pronounced "Vahv," and in this book the reader will notice that it is at times pronounced "Wahv." This choice of pronunciation is in deference to the more ancient Hebraic pronunciation of the ו, which in the past differentiated it from the pronunciation of the letter ב "Veht." The "W" sound for ו is possibly more indigenous to the aboriginal Hebrew, as it remains so in the Hebrew dialect of Jewish communities which have thrived in the Land of Israel and in neighboring regions uninterruptedly for millennia. These include — but are not limited to — the *Shom'ronim*, remnants of the northern tribes of Israel, and the Jews of Yemen.

All of these teachings and more combine to guide us with clues about ourselves, the unique auspiciousness of each moon cycle, and the magic of each of our life walk regardless of our religious or cultural backgrounds. In order to determine your birth month by the Hebraic lunar calendar reckoning, please visit: http://www.chabad.org/calendar/1000year_cdo/aid/6225/jewish/Date-Converter.htm, and enter your birth month, day and year into the area marked "Civil to Hebrew," then "Go," and your Hebrew birth date will appear.

The information in this book is not only an in-depth look at Kabbalistic astro mystery, but can be wonderfully beneficial when implemented in day to day practice in regards to the gateways of the seasons and to the calendar as well. Whether or not you were born under the particular moon you are reading about, each month wields a quality and numerous practical life lessons that you are welcome to draw from during that month. Exploring those life lessons during each month will prove to be a rich and soul-nurturing practice.

Let us now walk through these teachings and explore the magical mysteries of the Dance of Moon.

NOTES

1. 16th-century Rabbi Chayyim Vital in Volume 1 of *Etz Chayyim, Heychal Adam Kad'mon* 1:5.

2. *Talmud Bav'li, Berachot* 64a; *Shabbat* 156a-b.

3. *Talmud Bav'li, Shabbat* 75a.

4. 18th-century Rabbi Moshe Chayim Luzatto in *Derech Hashem* 2:7.

5. *Mishnah, Avot* 5:22.
6. *Midrash Shir Hashirim Rabbah* 5:3.
7. Midrash Pesikta Rabbatti 44:16.
8. *Mishnah, Avot* 2:4.
9. Genesis 1:2.
10. *Talmud Bav'li, Berachot* 33b.
11. *Midrash Shir HaShirim Rabbah* 6:15.
12. Exodus 13:4 and 23:15.
13. Deuteronomy 16:1.
14. 11th-century Rabbi Shlomo Yitzchaki [Rashi] on *Talmud Bav'li, Rosh Hashanah* 21a.
15. *Midrash Pirkei D'Rebbe Eliezer*, Ch. 6.
16. *Mishnah, Rosh Hashanah* 2:2.
17. First Kings 6:1.
18. Exodus 23:16.
19. First Kings 8:2.
20. *Talmud Bav'li, Rosh Hashanah* 11a.
21. First Kings 6:38.
22. *Talmud Yerushalmi, Rosh Hashanah* 6a.
23. *Mishnah, Rosh Hashanah* 1:1.
24. *Midrash B'reisheet Rabbah* 92:6.
25. Exodus 28:17-21.
26. *Talmud Bav'li, K'ree'tut* 6a.
27. Manuscript Parma — de Rossi 1221, folio 288b.
28. Zohar, Vol. 1, folio 20b.
29. Job 12:7-8.
30. *Sefer Yetzirah* 6:17.
31. Exodus 39:7.
32. Zohar, Vol. 1, folio 231a.

Chapter Two

Nee'sahn

(March 16–May 8)

Nee'sahn ניסן, meaning Miraculous
Attribute: Speech, Communication שיחה *see'chah*
Tribe: Reuvayn ראובן meaning "Behold! A son!"
Tribal Totem: Water מים *ma'yeem* whose quality is Mother of Life, and Other-Worldliness
Tribal Stone: Ruby אודם *O'dehm* whose quality is protection against miscarriage
Tribal Herb: Balsam צרי *tz'aree*
House: Life בית החיים *beyt ha'chayyim*
Zodiac: Lamb טלה *t'leh*
Letter: *hay* ה Window
Tribal Flag: אדום Red *e'do'm*, with image of a mandrake fruit
Tribal Direction: South, נגב *negev* "Cleansing," and דרום *da'rom* "Rising"

The Hebraic month of Nee'sahn is referred to in the Torah as *Cho'desh Ha'ah'vee'v* חודש האביב the Moon of Spring, or of the Renewal of the Grain Crop. Elsewhere in the Hebraic Scriptures it is known as the Moon of זיו *Zee'v*, Brilliance. It is also originally called חודש הראשון *Cho'desh Ha'Ree'shon,* or The First Month.[1] It was so called because the ancient Israelites were instructed to reckon their very first calendar month from the time of their exodus from enslavement in Egypt, the momentous occasion of their becoming an independent nation.[2] The Jewish people celebrate this event annually as Passover, which begins on the night of the fourteenth day of the Moon of Nee'sahn. Subsequent months were then originally named simply by their *proximity* to that event, Second Month, Third Month, Fourth Month, and so on. Prior to this period, then, Nee'sahn would have been considered the *Seventh* Month, since the Torah's reckoning of the beginning of human time is the Autumn month of Tish'ray, the moon of the Hebraic New Year. Therefore, Nee'sahn is the month during which Noah's Ark finally settled atop Mount Ararat, which is recorded to have occurred on "the Seventeenth Day of the Seventh Month."[3] That would also coincide this occasion with the Hebraic Festival of Liberation: Passover.

The word *Nee'sahn* is related to the Hebrew word for Miracle, נס *ness*, and at the same time is related to the word *Nee'sa'yon* נסיון, which translates as Test, or Challenge. Miracle is about transcending the natural order of things, the predictable patterns of life, the assumptions and presumptions, the status-quo. Similarly, challenge dares us to take steps across the threshold of the unknown next moment, to walk where we never thought we could; to shed what was, in order to enable the emergence of what could be, like the snake shedding its skin.

Nee'sahn is auspiciously gifted with the qualities of freedom and liberation, and also with the anxiety that often accompanies these. During this period of liberation from bondage, the Hebrew ancestors were vacillating between being freed up from 210 years of slavery and actually leaving Egypt, as well as the uncertainty of stepping into the unknown, into the desert, not knowing if there will be water, if there will be food, or if the journey ahead will actually bring them to their homeland and intact.

The miracle of what happened was great — Moses arriving, performing his miraculous feats in front of the Pharaoh, bringing us hope of redemption, all good. But we also felt challenged by the anxiety and fear and insecurity regarding survival in the immediate future. Slavery notwithstanding, Egypt had been our home for several centuries. At least here we had food and water, and shelter from the Sun — we had stability, even though it was harsh. The alternative sounded attractive, but at the same time, the process involved in that alternative felt intimidating.

So many uncertainties, so much anxiety, leading of course to frustration, anger, and in the process, the shattering of appreciation of the miracles we were witnessing daily through Moses, Aaron, and Miriam. We also wrestled with impatience over not knowing what was going to happen to us — will the miraculous continue? Will the Pharaoh finally give in and let us go? Will they throw the redeemers in jail along with our hopes? Will we be able to leave safely? Will we make it across the border before the Egyptians change their mind and come after us?

Perhaps you too have had such experiences, realizing your life may not be what you want it to be. At such times, you may feel enslaved by your own personal "Egypt." Egypt in the Hebrew vernacular, by the way, is *mitz'rayim* מצרים, related to and spelled exactly the same as the word *metza'rim* מצרים

for narrows or constriction. If you feel enslaved to a particular life situation that is keeping you from growing, improving, evolving; that is keeping you from being happy with who you are and what you do; or perhaps keeping you in a relationship or career that does not nurture you but rather drains you — then this is the month to evaluate your situation and prepare to liberate yourself. And in so doing, be prepared for the natural feeling of anxiety over leaving that which has been all too familiar and therefore safe and secure, albeit deadening or stifling. Fear of reaching blindly out to the unknown "next" while letting go of the security of what was, is to be expected, and the Miracle Month dares you to take the leap of faith and walk into the intimidating sea of uncertainty.

There is an oral tradition that the famous Red Sea (actually Sea of Reeds) did not really split for the fleeing Israelites until one man, Nach'shon ben Ami'nadav (literally: Snake Man son of My Benevolent People), stepped into the sea and continued walking until the waters reached his nostrils. Only *then* did it split.[4]

Nee'sahn is not only about the challenge of moving from being stuck to fluidity, from bondage to freedom. It is also the beginning of Spring, which brings the same kinds of anxiety as we wait to see whether the seeds of Winter will open up and the fruit of the Earth will emerge once again from the frozen soil of Winter. We planted our hopes in Summer and Autumn, and now as Nee'sahn arrives, we wonder whether those dreams, those seeds, will sprout forth, will become liberated from the realm of possibility and break through into the freedom of realization. And once they emerge, will they wilt shortly thereafter, or ripen? Will the grasses, the leaves, the flora coming forth at this time be short-lived due to a frost or strong winds or drastic change in temperature, or will they flourish toward maturity?

And so we work all this through in the ritual of Passover, or *Peh'sach* פסח — the very first festival our people were given while we were still in Egypt, preparing for our Springtime emergence, our liberation from the constrictions of Egypt. Again, you don't have to be Jewish to apply the underlying meanings behind these rites of liberation, nor do you have to be born in Nee'sahn. Basically, they involve three important steps:[5]

1. *Simplify.* The Israelites feasted only on מצה *matzoh*, the most basic and most simplified form of bread, comprised solely of flour and water. Water represents the force that moves seed toward fruition, potential and dream toward realization — wheat kernels toward wheat stalks. Flour represents the intermediate phase of that unfolding, of the evolution of wheat into bread. Now, add eggs and yeast and butter, etc., and you inflate it so much that you lose sight of the basics. Therefore, Passover celebrants refrain during Passover from eating enriched breads and cakes, and eat only *matzoh*, as a practice of restoring the consciousness of simplicity and basics in order to engage liberation. You cannot free yourself if you are weighed down by the superfi-

cial, if your heart, your truth, is veiled by too many layers of patterns and worries that keep you trapped.

Step One, then, is simplify. Identify what in your life weighs you down unnecessarily; what in your life dims your vision of a better You; what in your life prevents you from moving forward.

2. *Sacrifice.* Before leaving behind their 210 years of bondage, the Israelites were told to sacrifice. Sacrifice in Hebrew — קרבן *kor'ban* - is rooted in the Hebrew word for Nearness, קרוב *ka'rov*, which also translates as relative, as in family. Sacrifice is a gesture which demands of us that we give something up in order to draw near, approach closer to our personal truth. In bondage, we sacrifice our personal truth to the agenda or the desire of another. In liberation, we sacrifice that which stands in the way of our self-essence and our truth so that we might cross the chasm that separates us, that fragments us. In ancient times, when we sacrificed to Creator, we could only do so by bringing to the altar that into which we had invested our selves, our own personal blood, sweat and tears, our toil, our energy, our soul, whether from our flocks or from our fields.[6] This gesture was intended to free us of our tendency to become enslaved by our work, by our careers, our jobs. By surrendering the works of your labor, tokens of your achievements, you become freed of the chains that bind you to the desperation that constantly drives you. Instead you are reminded that it is not all your power and might that has accomplished all this, but that Creator has partnered with you all along in manifesting for you all that you so diligently strove for.[7] Sacrifice reminds you to step back from being driven by your work, and that not everything rests on your shoulders. As the second-century Rabbi Tar'fon put it, "The work is not upon you to complete; nor are you exempt from trying."[8]

Sometimes, your relatives and your family are sacrificed in the process of your self-liberation. Sometimes their preferences and priorities, and even their demands, are offered on the altar in the process of reclaiming your selfhood. The *ka'rov* becomes then the *kor'ban*. It doesn't mean you have to run away from home. It means rather that at times you need to remind those close to you that you too are an individual with rights to exist and to be honored as an independent creature. Like the ancient rabbis taught: "Every person is obliged to declare 'On my account alone was the universe created.'"[9]

Step Two, then is about Sacrifice. How prepared are you to sacrifice old patterns in your relationship, or in your career choices or friendships, in order to remove those factors which impede your connection with your Self? And are you willing to do so upon the altar, meaning in a way that is sacred, that liberates both you and others from unhealthy patterns.

3. *Bitterness.* The final ritual is that of מרור *ma'ror*. Along with sacrificing and simplifying, we add one more component to Nee'sahn's gift of liberation: Bitter Herbs. We ingest plants that are healthy for our bodies yet

very bitter for our taste buds, such as the horseradish root. This final phase of the rites of liberation is about feeling the pain as opposed to negating it or denying it. The ancient Israelites were instructed to add bitter herbs to their ceremonial Passover/Exodus feast to remind them that it is futile to simply leave their trauma behind in their flight from slavery. To do so would perhaps mean a successful escape, but not a successful liberation. If we don't face the trauma, the pain, the hurt in our lives, then we drag it all along with us as we purport to "go on" with our lives. Facing the pain, the guilt, the anxiety, as you move through the challenging gauntlet of your personal liberation, is crucial to the efficacy of that liberation. Grieving over what happened or over what had to happen for you to free yourself from your personal Egypt is as vital as the exodus itself. You want to make a clean break from what binds you, while allowing the imprint of what you gleaned from your experience to remain an integral part of the wisdom you carry.

Peh'sach פסח has several meanings. It is pronounced the same way as the Hebrew word for Doorway — *peh'sach* in Ashkenazic pronunciation פתח — albeit spelled slightly differently. Nee'sahn is our doorway. At the doorway, we hesitate, like our ancestors did in Egypt. Should we leave? Should we stay? Should we remain with what we already know, or should we dare to take a step toward something new and different? Should we stay in the silence of Winter, or should we dance forward in the drama of Spring?

Peh'sach also means "to leap," and that too is the message of this moon: don't linger, don't wait too long at the doorway, at the passageway to possibility, to transformation. Take a leap forward. Spring! Oftentimes you may find yourself lingering in the doorway of possibility, of change, but you're not sure it's the right time, or the right move, or even the right doorway. The eighteenth-century mystic, Rabbi Nachmon of Breslav taught that it matters not so much what road you take; it matters most that you take one, that you take a daring step onto whichever road rather than linger at the crossroads too long. Nor does it matter where you end up; what matters most is that once you get there, find something good to do there.[10] Or in the earlier words of the ancient ones: "Thus says God, 'Just do; and whatever it is that you find to do, it is pleasing unto me.'"[11]

Ironically, though, when we change the vowels for this Hebrew word *Peh'sach*, we get *Pee'say'ach*, which means "to limp"! So at the same time we are urged to leap forward in the Moon of Spring, at the threshold of redemption, we are also told of the cost involved: limping. Just like our ancestral father Jacob ended up with a limp after successfully overcoming the angel in combat.[12] When we dare leap over the hurdles that hinder our unfolding, we often pay a price. Our walk is not the same as it used to be. We might alienate a few friends, family members, co-workers, relationship partners, and so on. It costs to grow. It costs to emerge anew. But know that if this occurs, there is a possibility that those in your immediate circle will see the beauty of your new resonance and attempt to join you. Likewise, there may be new people who will show up in your life, who are on a parallel rung in the spiral of their own unfolding.

Every month has its particular quality, or *attribute*. The attribute of the Moon of Spring, is שיחה *see'chah*, *Communication*, or *Speech*. Back in Egypt, we communicated our anxiety, our impatience, in speech, in angry talk against the very person who gave his *all* to free us: Moses. [13] Communication is extremely challenging. It can make or break a relationship, ignite a war or foster peace. It was first invented by Snake, who is the equivalent of Trickster in our tradition. Snake in Hebrew is *Na'chash* נחש, which literally means "To Trick, or To Fool." Snake challenges us, calls our bluff, and tests our deepest convictions. In our creation story, Snake is the first creature to communicate, dialoguing with First Woman, Eve (*Chavah* חוה in Hebrew), and thereby eliciting response, and inventing the very first challenge to the very first humans. Communication is therefore associated with challenge, and appropriately the quality of Nee'sahn, as the word *Nee'sahn* — again — is also rooted in its cousin *nee'sa'yon*, which means test, challenge, and also experience. *Nee'sa'yon* therefore implies Drama — specifically the drama of life, which is all about experience, challenges, tests, miracles, leaping, limping — basically all the components involved in moving from stoicity or complacency to aliveness. Spring time is here!

Each moon in the Hebraic calendar is associated with one of the twelve tribes of the ancient Israelites. Nee'sahn being the first of the months is associated with Reuvayn ראובן, first of the tribes, eldest and firstborn of the family of Jacob and his wives. Reuvayn is the quiet elder, the diplomat. When his brothers scheme to rid themselves of their younger sibling Joseph, he intercedes and suggests that they place him in a pit, planning to return later to pull Joseph out and rescue him from their fatal plot. [14] Unfortunately, by the time he returns to help Joseph, Joseph has already been sold into slavery and carried off to Egypt. Reuvayn is devastated and rips his clothing in mourning. [15] From the start, he demonstrates a persona who is apart, who is thinking more clearly than the crowd. It is no wonder that his tribe was assigned the direction of South as their position in the configuration of the Israelites as they journeyed through the desert of Sinai following their exodus from Egypt. [16] South in Hebrew is דרום Da'rom, which means "Rising" — in Reuvayn's case, rising above the masses. Another word for South is נגב Negev, meaning "Cleanse," as in clear thinking, another trait of Reuvayn whose clear thinking does not allow him to blindly follow the majority decision of his brothers to harm Joseph. He is the fulfillment of the Torah's prohibition against submitting to the pressures of the crowd when you know they are in error. [17]

Reuvayn is of a complicated nature. Eventually, he loses his status to his younger brother Yehudah יהודה, Judah, who takes over the reins of leadership of the tribes. He withdraws after failing to save Joseph, and in a moment of weakness even has an affair with one of his father's half-wives.[18] Jacob had two wives, Rachel and Le'ah, and two half-wives, or in Hebrew *pee'lahg'sheem* פלגשים, literally "half-wives,"[19] meaning they were free to terminate the relationship whenever they wished without a divorce (like domestic partners or a living-together situation in our own times). His half-wives were Bil'hah בלהה and Zil'pah זלפה. Reuvayn had an affair with Bil'hah, who was also the mother of two of his paternal brothers, Dan דן and Naftalee נפתלי. So Reuvayn is somewhat on the outside of things as well as on the inside. On the one hand he withdraws into the shadows and disassociates himself from his brothers and their plot against Joseph, and on the other hand he chastises them for what they did.[20]

Reuvayn's descendants continue his patterns of being different, of living outside the community. Before the tribes reach the Land of Canaan after their forty-year desert trek following their exodus from Egypt, Reuvayn breaks rank again. This time his descendants inform Moses of their preference to settle in what is today Jordan, rather than cross over into the Promised Land. At the same time, the tribe pledges to assist the other tribes in resettling in Canaan, but they have no intentions of living there themselves.[21] Although they preferred the other side of the Jordan River, they still kept their promise to help the other tribes get settled in Canaan before returning to their newly-chosen homeland.[22]

Reuvayn's characteristics are probably a result of the intention that his mother Ley'ah לאה had when she first named him. She felt not as loved by Jacob as her sister Rachel רחל, and when she bore Jacob his first child, she experienced the birth and the extra attention it brought her from Jacob as a response from God to her anguish. So she called her son Reuvayn, "For God has *ra'ah b'an'yeey* — ראה בעניי — seen me in my anguish."[23] Reuvayn then is born from the place of aloneness, of feeling left out, yet a part of the family.

The tribal Totem assigned to Reuvayn is Water *ma'yeem* מים — whose quality is Mother of Life, because it was the primordial element created at the very beginning. It represents Other-Worldliness, since it is an atmosphere in which we humans cannot survive, on the one hand, and *without* which we cannot survive, on the other hand. Water is the force that calls forth what lies dormant within the Earth, within us, within our dreams. Water is the conjurer of fruition, of actualization. She is the primal mother of Creation, from which Earth emerged.[24] She embodied all of the potential of primeval Creation and called it forth into being, and without her, nothing lives. She is also the power of cleansing, of emptying, and of renewal, as in the ritual of immersing in the ritual pool we call מקוה Mikveh.

Each tribe was represented by a particular gem stone that was sewn into the breastplate of the High Priest. For the tribe of Reuvayn it is the *o'dehm*

אודם — the Ruby.[25] The o'dehm helps us to protect ourselves against miscarriage, meaning also that it helps us to protect ourselves from mistranslating other people's communication or reactions. Sometimes we have trouble following through with what we are trying to birth, difficulty holding onto it for an extended period of time, for the amount of time it needs in order to manifest, which demands patience. This is especially true in relationships, where we may become impatient with the very differing pace of our partner and how long it takes for them to meet us where *we* are. In Nee'sahn some 3300 years ago, we struggled with this very same issue, holding on long enough to the hope of liberation while challenged with the obstacles of doubt and anxiety about the efficacy of the promised redemption.

O'dehm is spelled in Hebrew the same way as you would spell the Hebrew word for Human אדם (*ah'dahm*) or Red אדום (*eh'do'm*) simply by changing the vowels. The root of this word is *Adamah* אדמה, or Earth, and the particular quality of Earth that is permeable, having to do with shaping, such as clay. The *o'dehm* stone therefore represents the courage to shape, to create your own destiny, even when it differs from what is expected of you by others. This theme is, again, demonstrated by the story of the corresponding tribe of Reuvayn, the tribe of the Moon of Nee'sahn, the tribe that deviates from the national dream of return to the ancestral homeland and instead opts for another land on the other side of the Jordan. This is the gift of being Human. This is the gift of that part of the Earth that is clay. This is the passion, the red burning passion that flows through us as it flows through the Earth in Spring, calling forth to realization the dreams that were seeded deep inside the Earth. Likewise, in Nee'sahn we call forth from the place of our own life passions the dreams and hopes seeded deeply within ourselves.

When you are feeling the need for a little help in softening your baked-in Earthy self, your etched-in-stone situation, take a ruby stone in your right hand. The right side implies uninhibited flow, or חסד *Chessed*. Hold it in your hand until you feel the warmth of your blood blending with the warmth of the stone so that its life force and yours join as one. Then close your eyes and inhale deep within your being from the stone through your hand up your arm into your heart and into your heart of hearts, with the intent of unclogging your own life flow to enable it to stream once again and move you into joy and liberation.

Each moon also has its own herb, corresponding to the plants that made up the ingredients of the sacred incense offering in ancient times, known as the *keh'to'reht* קטורת.[26] For Nee'sahn, the herb is the *tza'ree* צרי or Balsam. The word *tza'ree* is related to the Hebrew word for constrictiveness or narrowness — *tz'ar* צר. Balsam is about narrowing something down to its most basic, most fundamental power or quality, removing all the fluff, all the outer trimmings that conceal our deepest truths, and leaving us naked with our authenticity. In the sacred incense mix, this powerful herb stripped the other herbs and plants of their external garb so that the blend became that much more potent, left only with the essence of each plant and its primary quality and life force. This is what happens when we dare to liberate ourselves from patterns involving other people, when we dare to move through those three Passover rites mentioned earlier. We not only strip ourselves down to the core of our personal truth, but we end up doing this for other involved parties as well, just like Balsam does to the other sacred herbs.

This herb is therefore helpful to us when we feel overwhelmed, overshadowed by all that is coming at us in life that make our problems appear larger than ourselves. The *tza'ree* herb shrinks our world somewhat so that we can restore our self-essence and remember that we are larger than our problems. As such, it corresponds to the Month of Nee'sahn, the Moon of Spring, the time of the Exodus, all of which is about emerging from the constrictiveness of the frozen Earth of Winter and the suffocating bondage of our personal "Egypt."

Balsam was also used in shamanic journeying to bring back someone who might have gotten stuck in a journey.[27] It would strip that person of all superficiality, all ego, and reduce the person to their bare essential self, thereby dislodging them from the realm in which they might have gotten stuck. The balsam was grounded into its own bare essence, its oil, which was then poured onto virgin sheep wool wrapped around the twig of an acacia tree or cedar tree, and then applied on the thigh of the one stuck in the journey. If you feel stuck in the doorway of your transformation, get some balsam oil and apply it over that part of your body where you feel the most anxiety about your next move, be it your heart, your gut, your head, etc.

The key in learning how to ride the waves of your life unfolding, rather than floundering in the tide, is to visit the בית *bah'yeet*, the particular mystery House associated with your month. The House for Nee'sahn is *Bayt Ha'Chayyimm* בית החיים the House of Life, of Aliveness. This is where we are challenged to bring ourselves into, to dwell in, the realm of aliveness, not allowing all of our issues and anxieties to deaden us, to numb us from the gift of being.

In Nee'sahn, Moses challenged us to step into the Red Sea (Sea of Reeds or *yahm soof* ים סוף), to step into the water, the very Totem of Nee'sahn, to dare engage the uncertainty, to embrace the Mother of Aliveness, Water — the first element of Genesis in our Creation story. In the word for water, מים *ma'yeem* — originally spelled מימ (there were no ending letters in the ancient writ) — the letters represent a womb followed by a seed followed in turn by another womb: מ which is symbolic of womb, then י, which is shaped like a seed, and means "contained hand," then מ again. Water, is then symbolic of the eternal phases of our unfolding into Life. We are always a seed, always a *yod*, the letter which literally translates as "contained hand" — grasping within it seed of possibility which we then grow and sprout to fruition in the wombs of opportunity across many lifetimes.

House of Life may sound very auspicious and invigorating, but as a Nee'sahn child, you know better. You know first-hand how being in Life is an amazing challenge, as there is so much in the world and in your personal life that distracts you from *being* in life. The more alive you feel, having been born during the Moon of Spring, the more sensitive you may be, and the more you might feel the angst of all that frustrates or outright impedes your connection to the magic and ever-flowing flux of life. You are the grass reaching toward the sky from the constrictiveness of Earth, the bud on the tree limb eagerly and impatiently pushing against the slow pace of life in order to unfold and blossom. Your desires move you toward unbridled and un-tempered celebration and life dance against the backdrop of forces with agendas of tempering and directing you.

Your corresponding Shadow House is the House of Women — *Bayt Ha'na'sheem* בית הנשים. If your house is the House of Life, your passions, your excitement, your keen awareness, are already in flux, spinning, flowing, dancing freely and haphazardly without any specific choreography. House of Life sits on the right side of the Sephirotic Tree, the proverbial tree that carries the sap, so to speak, of the Divine Intent for all existence to be and to become. The right side of this tree — also known as the Tree of Life — is the place of חסד *Chessed*, unbridled, uninhibited flow. The House of Women, on the other hand, sits on the *left* side of the Sephirotic Tree, the place of the quality of גבורה *Gevurah*, the tempering force, the guiding and directing force that often frustrates our inclination toward being carefree. *Gevurah* inhibits our impulsiveness since its intention is not just to bring life out of seed but also to *direct* it and guide it — to *raise* the child, not only to *birth* the child; to create an intelligent designed universe, not one of chaos and randomness. Chaos is how our Creation story begins, and then the feminine force hovers over the primal waters,[28] directing, guiding, *intending* the chaos — the free-flow of primal creation — toward an intelligent, intentional design and out-come.

One example of the clash of House of Life and House of Women is portrayed in the Biblical story of King David. After retrieving the Ark of the Covenant from the hands of the Philistines, David celebrated by dancing wildly down the streets of Jerusalem dressed only in a loincloth.[29] No sooner did he arrive home that evening when he was chastised by Mee'chahl, one of his wives, who criticized him for acting so care-free in public:[30] a perfect story of the clash of *Chessed*, unbridled expression, and *Gevurah*, the tempering force that tends to seize what is unstructured and *give* it structure. We also see this in the difference between the energies of the Pharaoh's daughter, who gives Moses a name connoting flow, משה *Moshe*, and Moses' mother who gives him a name connoting structure, אביגדור *Avig'dor*. Yet, the empowerment gifted to him by both women, by both *Gevurah* and *Chessed*, creates in him the balance of both, as both qualities were needed in leading the people and in guiding the people.

To deal wholesomely with your Shadow House, the House of Women, it would be helpful to explore the feminine and incorporate its gifts into your House of Aliveness without allowing it to stifle or hinder your nature. Welcome instead its gift of intended design to help bring your seeds of dream and hope to fruition in wholesome ways.

Like other ancient systems, the Hebrew moons, too, have their Zodiac qualities. For Nee'sahn it is the Lamb, the *t'leh* טלה in Hebrew. Lamb represents innocence, purity, letting go of all the givens and definitions placed on us in life and restoring our simplicity, our essential innocent self, the prerequisite to new unfolding, to new encounters. Lamb means stepping back from our judgmental self and bringing forth our open-hearted self, so that we might have the fortitude to do what is required of us in the moment; to cross the sea that lies between our past and our future, between the place of being stuck and the place of fresh possibilities. The Torah therefore often describes our ancestors as seeing things completely fresh, completely new, using these words: "And he lifted up his eyes and he saw — *va'yee'sa ay'nahv va'yar'* וישא עיניו וירא,"[31] meaning he no longer saw the same thing in the same way, but lifted his way of seeing above the way in which he'd been accustomed to seeing. Lamb challenges us to see our loved ones not continuously in the same way, with the same assumptions with which we saw them and experienced them yesterday, but to do so anew, daily.

As described earlier, every month also has its association with a particular letter in the Hebrew alphabet system. For Nee'sahn it is the letter *Hay* ה, which means Window. Windows are passageways through which we not only see out from within, but also see in from without. It is the merging of our external self and internal self. It challenges us to live with awareness of who we are in essence when we are in our private life and who we are in essence when we are in our *public* life, and to merge the two in harmonious union. Window in Kabbalistic terms represents each our capacity to see beyond the obvious, to look beyond our limited perspectives to behold the magic of the larger picture of life around us, and to experience the mystery so skillfully camouflaged within everything and everyone.[32]

NOTES

1. Esther 3:7.
2. Exodus 12:2.
3. Genesis 8:4.
4. *Midrash Shir Hashirim Zuta* 2:1.
5. *Mishnah, Pesachim* 10:5.
6. Leviticus 1:2 and 2:1.

7. Deuteronomy 8:17-18.
8. *Mishnah, Avot* 2:16.
9. *Mishnah, Sanhedrin* 4:5.
10. *See'chot Ha'RaN*, Ch. 85.
11. *Talmud Bav'li, B'chorot* 17b.
12. Genesis 32:35.
13. Exodus 5:21.
14. Genesis 37:21-22.
15. Genesis 37:29.
16. Numbers 2:10.
17. Exodus 23:2.
18. Genesis 35:32.
19. *Talmud Bav'li, Sanhedrin* 21a.
20. Genesis 42:22.
21. Numbers, Chapter 32.
22. Joshua 22:9.
23. Genesis 29:32.
24. Genesis 1:9.
25. Exodus 28:17.
26. Exodus 30:7-9; *Talmud Bavli, K'ree'tut* 6a.
27. Vol. 1 of *Batei Midrashot, Pirkei Heychalot* Rabbati 20:3.
28. Genesis 1:2.
29. Second Samuel 6:14.
30. Second Samuel 6:20.
31. E.g., Genesis 18:2, 22:4, 22:13, 24:63, 33:1. 43:29; Joshua 5:13; Judges 19:17.
32. Zohar, Vol. 3, folio 184b.

Chapter Three

Iyyar

(April 10-June 8)

Iyyar אייר , meaning "breaking through of the Light"
Attribute: Thought and Imagination הרהור *hir'hur*
Tribe: Shim'on שמעון meaning "My anguish was heard"
Tribal Totem: Canyon נקיק *nah'keek*, shelter/fortress/protection from storminess
Tribal Stone: Topaz פטדה *peeteh'dah* whose quality is quieting of emotions, of the heart
Tribal Herb: Onycka (cloves [*Talmud Bav'li, Keritut* 6b]) צפורן *tzee'po'rehn*
House: Prosperity בית הממון *bayt ha'ma'mo'n*
Zodiac: Buffalo שור *sho'r*
Letter: *vahv* ו Hook
Tribal Flag: ירוק Green *ya'ro'k*, with image of Village of Shechem
Tribal Direction: South, נגב *negev* "Cleansing," and דרום *da'rom* "Rising"

Iyyar means "breaking through of the light" and implies great passion and spirit force that is dormant and waiting for the right opportunities to emerge, to break forth "Like the going forth of the Sun in its power," as Devorah the Prophetess put it in her famous song.[1] Or, as King David put it: "Like a bridegroom emerging from beneath the wedding canopy, dancing joyfully like a warrior, conjuring his potential to run forth."[2] Iyyar, writes the 18th-century Rebbe Nachmon of Breslav, is the most auspicious time for collecting the most potent plants for medicinal purposes.[3] It is a healing moon, a moon that empowers the forces of healing that lay dormant within the Earth, calling those forces to the surface and to their most optimal potency.

Iyyar is also the month in which we celebrate the concept of *Pesach Shay'nee* שני פסח, Second Passover. This was a special gift given to us in the desert during our exodus to teach us that it's never ever too late to celebrate or acknowledge something that is past, that we may have missed. During the Exodus journey we were told that everyone had to celebrate the Passover on the same day, the 14th day of the moon of Nee'sahn in the time of the full moon of the Moon of Spring. Every Israelite had to participate. But there happened to be some of us who had been busy tending to the dead at that time and since we were ritually unclean from burying the dead, we could not participate in these sacred rites on that very day. God then tells Moshe (Moses) that those of us who couldn't participate in the Pesach (Passover) rituals on the appointed day — whether for reasons of ritual impurity or coming from afar — could make it up on the same day in the *following* month, the month of Iyyar.[4]

In the Torah, Iyyar is referred to as the Second Month, as all the months in early biblical times were named by number in relationship to their proximity to the month in which the Exodus from Egypt took place. The second month, Iyyar, was also the moon in which the Cloud of Glory finally lifted from the Ark of the Covenant, signaling to the people that they could now resume their journey following their encampment.[5] Until then, the people were settled in Sinai as the Revelation continued and the construction of the Tabernacle, or משכן *mish'kahn,* continued. The Cloud of Glory signaled to the people when it was okay to pick up and go, and when it was necessary to settle down and pitch camp. When the cloud settled on the Ark of the Covenant, it meant we had to stop our journey and camp out. When it lifted, it meant we were to resume our journey.[6] The moon of Iyyar, then, teaches us to know when to move and when to fold up and wait. It is about right timing.

Iyyar was also the month in which the building of the First Temple — Solomon's Temple — was begun.[7] And surprisingly enough, it was the month in which the building of the *Second* Temple had begun as well, centuries later, following our return to Israel from our exile in Babylon and Persia.[8] It would appear therefore that Iyyar also represents new beginnings as well as restoration of what is lost. Again we have the theme of "It's never too late." It's never too late to start fresh, and it's never too late to start again with that which didn't work out the *first* time.

The particular attribute or quality that Iyyar represents is הרהור *hir'hur,* thought, thinking, and reasoning. Thinking something through before we leap into action. People born in Iyyar tend to spend a lot of time in their minds, thinking, contemplating, figuring things out in their heads before actually implementing. The shadow side of this, of course, is the often difficult process of translating thought into action once one is steeped in thought for a long time. Yet, Iyyar also empowers us to "break through" like the meaning of the word Iyyar itself: "Breaking through of the light."

This hesitation before action, this calm before the storm, is mirrored in our Creation story, where the primordial universe is described as chaotic, formless, dark, while the Spirit of Elo'heem was hovering over the waters of creation,[9] water representing the force that calls creation into being, calls what is dormant into fruition. And so, God is described as hovering, hesitating. And then suddenly: "And Elo'heem declared, 'Let the light *become*!'"[10] In other words, let the light that already was,[11] but only in thought, only in potential, only in the place of idea and dream…let it now manifest; let it break through!

So Iyyar gifts us with both the quality of thinking, birthing ideas, strategizing, as well as with the quality and courage to crack the shell open so that what we *think* also *becomes*, and what we dream manifests.

אייר Iyyar corresponds to the tribe of Shim'on, second son of Jacob and Leah. Shim'on's archetype is one of zeal, and "chutzpah," daring to break out of the mold, like light emerging from darkness. His power lies in thought, in הרהור *hir'hur*, the attribute assigned to this moon. He is quick in his thought, in his decisiveness, and therefore also quick to act — sometimes *too* quick. His tribe was assigned the direction of South as their position in the configuration of the Israelites as they journeyed through the desert of Sinai following their exodus from Egypt.[12] South in Hebrew is דרום Da'rom, which means "Rising." Not unlike his brother Reuvayn, Shim'on rises above the others in his zeal, as we shall see later. The other word for South, נגב Negev, meaning "Cleanse," as in Clarity, also fits Shim'on whose way of thinking is so clear that there is no room for "ifs" and "buts," let alone "second thoughts," and his superior clarity takes him to dangerous situations, as we will see in the unfolding of his story.

His mother named him Shim'on שמעון as in "My pain has been heard" — *Shema* שמע related to hear, listen, and עון *o'n* related to anguish, pain. Ley'ah suffered from her husband Ya'akov's lack of romantic attention to her, since his energies in that arena were directed more toward her sister Ra'chel. She had hoped that maybe by bearing Ya'akov children, he would be drawn closer to her. So when her first son was born, she called him Reuvayn, as if to say: "God has seen my anguish, because now my man will love me!"[13] But it didn't help improve matters too much, so she called this second son Shim'on because — as she put it: "God has heard that I am not loved, and has given me this one, too.[14] So with her first son — who represents the first month of Nee'sahn — she speaks of God seeing: "God has seen my anguish," and with her second son — who represents the second month of Iyyar — she speaks of God *hearing*: "God has heard that I am not loved." Nee'sahn, the first month, is the Moon of Spring,[15] the moon when we came out of bondage in Egypt, the moon when the Earth frees up the growth of grasses and plants which begin to emerge into the open air and blossom — Spring Time. As such, Nee'sahn is appropriately the Moon of *Seeing*, when we are attracted visually to the greening that happens, the budding, the flowering — the emergence of beauty in shape and color. And Iyyar is the Moon of *Listening*. Now that the initial excitement of Spring with all of its visuals has receded some, it is time to listen, to shut our eyes and hear the *sounds* that accompany the springing forth of the gifts of the Earth: the song of birds, the symphony of frogs, cicadas, etc.

Shim'on knows no diplomacy. Only action. He lacks patience for the unfolding of process. He is wild, but focused. He is canyon, a solid fortress of defense from the winds of others. When the winds of Sh'chem son of Cha'mor, Prince of the Chee'vites, sweeps his sister Deenah away, he reacts immediately and with urgency along with his brother Ley'vee, destroying Sh'chem and recovering their sister.[16] His zeal for protection is so intense that one oral tradition has it that Deenah refused to leave her captors unless Shim'on promised to marry her.[17] It was the only way she would ever feel safe again after her ordeal. Even though her brother Ley'vee was also involved in her rescue, she nevertheless was more drawn to the protective quality of Shim'on.

Shim'on is often described as hot-headed because of his and his brother Ley'vee's overzealous response to the abduction of their sister. But when you read the story carefully, you will see that while their reaction resulted in severe and hot-headed consequences, their response itself at first was anything *but* that. When they first heard about the incident with Deenah, they cooled their emotions. They did not run out to the village to destroy it. They slowed down, made a plan, a scheme that took days, perhaps weeks to unfold.

Sh'chem fell in love with his victim and he, together with his father, Cha'mor, approached Deenah's family to request a match. Deenah's brothers responded and informed the two Chee'vites that their clan cannot intermarry with non-Hebrews unless their males ritually circumcise themselves. They said this as a way of discouraging the match. But Sh'chem and his father chose to circumcise themselves along with all the men in their village, to become one with the Hebrew clan so that Sh'chem could marry Deenah and so that they could increase their wealth. Of course, the brothers had no intention of allowing that to happen, for the honor of their sister. So when three days had passed since the mass circumcision of the male Chee'vite villagers, and the Chee'vites were still weakened from their circumcision, Shim'on and Ley'vee rode in and massacred all the males.[18] Because of their zealous love for their sister Deenah, and the extreme reaction they had in her honor, the Torah describes them alone as Deenah's brothers.[19]

The brazenness of the archetype of Shim'on is demonstrated centuries later during a tragic episode in the desert journey following the Exodus from

Egypt. When the Midianite prophet Bil'ahm fails to curse the Israelites as they pass through the land of Moab, the Midianites and Moabites both send their daughters to seduce the Israelites into worshiping and sacrificing to their deities. Moses is at his wit's end and totally distraught about what is happening to his people. And if that isn't enough, along comes the leader of the tribe of Shim'on, arm in arm with a Midianite woman, and the two make love in front of Moses' tent out of spite! [20]

Thus, the chutzpah of Shim'on was alive and well even centuries later. Consequently, Shim'on becomes the only tribe of the twelve that is deprived of national leadership throughout ancient Jewish history. As we discover in the Biblical Book of Judges, each of the tribes would have their turn with the election by Divine initiation of one of their own as chief of *all* the tribes. The only exclusion was the tribe of Shim'on. [21] The danger in this characteristic in terms of leadership is quite obvious. Leadership is no position for over-reactive people. Nevertheless, Shim'on's descendants go on to become teachers, sublimating their zealousness into zeal for study and educating. [22]

The Totem for the tribe of Shim'on, or Iyyar, is Fortress, or in the Earthly sense, Canyon נקיק *nah'keek* whose quality is shelter and protection from storminess, as well as revealing the mysteries of the depths, of the abyss, the mysteries of the heart and guts of the Earth, where the God Presence in the physical universe is most deeply manifested. The Torah tells us that during a vision experience, God tells Moses: "I am the Infinite One, who dwells in the guts of the Earth." [23] The canyon serves as a shelter from stormy winds, again, holding back unbridled forces, protecting from being swept away by impulse. The canyons are the Earth's revelation of herself, showing her heart, her deepest self, opening her arms to receive us, to embrace us, nurture us, protect us and shelter us. Deep in the Judean Desert, one can walk for miles without any sign of foliage or water. Then one comes to the canyons, and as one descends into these canyons, one discovers pools of clear cool water, and an abundance of vegetation, as well as caves for shelter.

The sacred stone worn on the breastplate of the ancient high priest of Israel that corresponded with the tribe of Shim'on is the פטדה *pee'teh'dah*, or Topaz, whose quality is about the quieting of emotions, of the heart. In the Kabbalah, the Topaz is described as the "Stone of the Right Side" of the Sephirotic Tree, the side of active flow, like the heart. [24] It therefore responds to, is drawn to, the forces that flow, such as Love, Prosperity, Blessing, Gift, and so on, keeping these in steady flow mode as opposed to overflow mode.

The Sacred Herb for this moon is the Onycka, or צפורן *tzee'po'rehn,* from the Hebrew word for Bird — צפור *Tzee'por* which in turn is rooted etymologically in the Hebraic word מצפצף *meh'tzahf'tzehf,* the word for chirping and other sounds of nature, even for the sound that waves make in the ocean. [25] This herb is thus related to song and chant. The word *tzee'po'rehn* is also related to the word צפרנים *tzee'por'nah'yim,* literally "nails" as in fingernails,

since the herb, a clove-like plant is, in its raw state, shaped very much like a
nail. It therefore has to do with the quality of grasping, holding onto something like the talons of an eagle. It has the power to capture and grasp firmly
onto the qualities of any other plant it is smoked with, merging its own
qualities and aroma with those of the accompanying plant. It was used to
seize what was harmful in a sick person and draw it out, like an eagle
swooping down upon its prey and seizing it with its talons.

צפורן *tzee'po'rehn* is about visioning the Beyond, aiding one in meditation
or shamanic journeying to move one's spirit body into the Beyond, into the
Universe of Mystery. It opens what is referred to in some traditions as the
"Third Eye," or in our tradition עינא דשכלא *ey'na deh'seech'la* — the Mind's
Eye, enabling us to see beyond this world, beyond the Known Universe. In
the blend of the Sacred Incense, this herb translated the others from their
physical, Earthly manifestations to their spirit roots in the Beyond, in the
Universe of Mystery.

The Realm or House associated with the moon of Iyyar is בית הממון *Bayt
Ha'ma'mo'n*, or House of Prosperity. Literally, ממון *ma'mon* usually implies
money. Money is a powerful force in our lives. It drives us. It flings open the
doors of Want with such force that it is difficult to pull those doors back and
be satisfied with what we have in hand. "Love money," wrote Solomon, "and
be never satisfied with money"[26] — meaning, it is often not enough. "Who is
the wealthy one?" asked the second-century Ben Zoma, "the one who is
satisfied with what he has"[27] — meaning, not overwhelmed by wanting more
and more and more. Not driven.

The power of money is so great that it is believed to be of a spiritual
nature at its core, virtually a part of the physical embodiment of our very
soul! The sixteenth-century Rabbi Yehudah Loew of Prague [MaHaRaL]
explained it this way:

> The human is basically comprised of four parts, (1) the body, (2) the soul, (3)
> the mind, and (4) money. For although money is not actually a part of the
> person himself, it is an integral part of [the *Gestalt* of] a person since it is his
> life-sustenance, and it is for him often more precious than his own person
> [people risk their very lives for money!].[28]

It therefore comes as no surprise that the ancient rabbis taught: "One who
steals so much as a פרוטה *p'rutah* (like a penny) from someone, it is as if they
have taken away that person's *soul*."[29]

The love of money, however, is not frowned upon in our tradition. Since
it is a spiritual force — so much so that we associate it with the composite of
a person, side by side with their soul and body — the ancients noted that the
tzadikim, the holy righteous ones, often cherished their money even *more* so
than they would their own persons.[30] The difference is in motive. Cherishing

money for the purpose of sustaining ourselves is a good thing, a spiritual practice. Cherishing money for the sake of accumulation alone is a dead end pursuit and is self-destructive.

The Talmud tells us an interesting story about Alexander the Great of Macedonia:

> When Alexander conquered the world, he was not satisfied until he had conquered the entire world. And so he took his conquest to the ends of the Earth, until there was no place left to conquer but Paradise. Arriving at the gates to Paradise, he demanded entry, but was denied. Not wanting to return a failure and empty-handed, he requested at least some kind of token, a souvenir, so he could boast of having been to Paradise. The gates opened slightly and an eyeball rolled out toward his feet. Curious, and wishing to evaluate the value of the eyeball, he ordered his servants to set up a weight scale and had them fill one side with heaps of gold and silver. He then placed the eyeball on the other side and it easily outweighed the gold and silver. Puzzled, he returned to the sages of Israel and asked them for an explanation. They said to him: "This is the eyeball of a human being, and as such, it is never satisfied with what it sees." Unconvinced, Alexander asked the sages to prove their point. "Take a little bit of Earth," they told him, "and cover the eyeball with it." This he did, and immediately the scales tipped to the side of the gold and silver. [31]

The Shadow Moon for Iyyar is the month of Chesh'von. It is the only month in the Hebrew calendar that has neither celebration nor commemoration. It is somewhat of a dead month. And sure enough, its house is the House of Death, בית המות *bayt ha'mah'veht.*

Coming from the House of Money, the Iyyar child is pitted against death in the sense of denial. When we have money, we are often inclined to put it away, save it for later, leave it for the future — all of which negates our sense of death, of our mortality, our finiteness. For in fact, we could die tomorrow and we would not have benefited from the gift of our money.

"If you have money," the 11th-century Rabbi Shlomo Yitzchaki [Rashi] wrote, "pleasure yourself with it, lest you die and end up not having derived any benefit from it. So do not wait until tomorrow. This world is like a party, so feast yourself on what is here, for tomorrow it will be gone. For death does not wait. It comes upon a person suddenly." [32] Obviously, the trick is balance. Learn to save for the future, and enjoy the present as well.

For the Iyyar child, this is often a challenge, coming from the House of Money. While money contributes to the quality of living, it also contributes to a lot of anxiety, worry, concern, and in a way has the potential to *drain* life rather than *sustain* life. And then there is, of course, the tragic fact that the obsession with money and its power has probably wreaked more havoc and death in the world throughout human history than most anything else.

The Zodiac for Iyyar is the שור *shor*, or Buffalo (not the American species, but the sort indigenous to North Africa and the Middle East). The attribute of Buffalo has to do with family ties, being a herd animal. The Buffalo, in Jewish teachings, is the keeper of the West, of מערב *ma'arav*,[33] the place of blending, since the color of Buffalo and of West is black, and black is the admixture, the blending, of all the colors. West is also where day encounters night, where light encounters darkness, where life encounters death, and therefore it is also the place of healing since healing takes place at the intersection of life and death. Therefore, the angelic keeper of the West is none other than רפאל Rafa'el, the angel of healing.

The Hebrew letter associated with Iyyar is the ו *Wahv*, which means Hook, and translates literally as "and" since it hooks what was, to what is to be. Therefore, in itself, it implies the magic of the moment.

Hook is also the antithesis to infiniteness, as it represents hooking us into the finite, into what the *wahv* literally means: "And." "And" belongs in the realm of time, space, and matter, connecting one moment to the next in a steady, ongoing stream, each moment separated from the one before and from the one pending. The ו is also *shaped* like a hook, linking past with future across the mystery of moment — all of which requires great faith and trust, faith in the mystery that moves the conspicuous, trust in the process that carries us to the next moment across the waves of uncertainty into the unknown next step.

NOTES

1. Judges 5:31.
2. Psalms 19:6.
3. *Likuttei MoHaRaN* , No. 277, para. 2 and Ibid, *Tanina* 1:11.
4. Numbers 9:10-11.
5. Numbers 10:11.
6. Numbers 9:17-23.
7. Second Chronicles 3:2.
8. Ezra 3:8.
9. Genesis 1:2.
10. Genesis 1:3.
11. Zohar, Vol. 1, folio 45b.
12. Numbers 2:12.
13. Genesis 29:32.
14. Genesis 29:33.
15. Exodus 13:4.
16. Genesis 34:25.
17. *Midrash B'reisheet Rabbah* 80:11.
18. Genesis, Chapter 34.
19. Genesis 34:25 — see also commentary of Rashi there.
20. Numbers 25:6 and 14.
21. *Otsar HaMidrashim, Pinchas ben Ya'ir, Keta* 8.
22. *Otsar Midrashim, Yaakov Ah'vee'nu, Keta* 13.
23. Exodus 8:18.
24. *Hak'damat Tikunay HaZohar*, folio 10a.
25. *Ba'tay Medra'sho't*, Vol. 2, 46:5; *Otzar Hamedrashim, Shlomo Hamelech, Keta* 6.
26. Ecclesiastes 5:9.

27. *Mishnah Avot* 4:1.

28. *Netivot Olam*, Vol. 1, folio 165, *Netiv Gemilut Chassadim*, Chapter 5.

29. *Talmud Bav'li, Baba Kama* 119a.

30. *Talmud Bav'li, Sotah* 12a.

31. *Talmud Bav'li, Tamid* 32b.

32. Rashi on *Talmud Bav'li, Eruvin* 58a.

33. *Midrash Bamid'bar Rabbah* 2:9; see also 13th century Rabbi Yitzchak of Akko in *M'irat Einayim, Bamidbar*, para. 2.

Chapter Four

See'vahn

(May 10-July 8)

See'vahn סיון, meaning "muddy"
Attribute: Attraction משיכה *m'shee'chah*
Tribe: Ley'vee לוי meaning "borrowed"
Tribal Totem: *Urim V'Tumim* אורים ותמים Oracle of Clarifications
Tribal Stone: Emerald ברקת *bo'reket* whose quality is refraction of Divine light
Tribal Herb: Galbanum חלבונה *chal'vo'nah*
House: Fellowship בית האחים *bayt ha'ah'cheem*
Zodiac: Twins תאומים *t'oo'meem*
Letter: *zah'yeen* ז Weapon
Tribal Flag: White *lavan* לבן, Black *shachor* שחור, Red *e'do'm* אדום, with image of the Oracle
Tribal Direction: Central, אמצעי *em'tza'ee,* "Strengthen"

סיון *See'vahn* literally means "muddy" as in the blend of opposites, the merging of Earth and water, wet and dry, female and male, the blend necessary to conjure the life force of the planted seed into its ultimate fruition, into actualization. It is the moon of chaos, when everything becomes muddled, not so clear, but is yet spurred by that very chaos into clarity, into the process of directed unfolding. After all, in our Creation story, we read in the very beginning how the primary force behind the Genesis of all existence is Chaos.[1] Sure enough, See'vahn usually follows the rainy season that comes with Spring, leaving the land messy, muddy. Mud has dual symbolism. On the one hand it is messy and chaotic. On the other hand, it is the magical

33

brew of Earth and water that is necessary for germinating what has been
seeded and coaching it to fruition.

See'vahn is the doorway to Summer, the moon of the first blossoming.
The Hebrew word for Summer, קיץ *ka'yeetz*, is related to the word, קיץ *kee'tz*,
for "awaken," as this is the season when Nature is completely awake, fully in
blossom and peaking with her colors, shapes, and aroma. This is a moon,
then, which calls forth the total realization of our faculties to a full awakening.

It is therefore in See'vahn that we celebrate *Shavu'ot* שבועות, the day we
experienced our collective Revelation at Mount Sinai about 3,300 years ago.
So it is also the month in which we blossomed as a people, as a nation. The
Torah brought us both experiences of perplexity (mud) and fruition. The
ancient rabbis asked: Why was the Torah given in See'vahn? Because
See'vahn according to the Judaic Zodiac is the Moon of Twins, of תאומים
t'oo'meem,[2] and the Torah is Gemini in nature, not absolute with only a
single way of interpreting her wisdom but rather *relative,* with *many* ways of
interpreting her wisdom — sometimes even in completely contradictory
ways.[3]

The attribute of this month is *Attraction*. Attraction can also at times
imply *distraction*, since distraction, too, is attractive. Attraction in the Hebraic sense is described as "being pulled," which is the literal meaning of the
Hebrew word for it — משיכה *m'shee'chah*. It is a completely different way of
looking at the concept of attraction. On one level, when we are attracted to
something, we are drawn *toward* it. On another level, when we are attracted
to something it could be that we are being pulled *by* it. The attribute of
attraction is therefore a dual concept, a double-edged sword, so to speak. It
challenges us with the following introspective question: Are you drawn to
something or to someone because of what you yourself seek, desire, long
for? Or arc you drawn because of the magnetic pull of the very thing or
person you find yourself fascinated by. Is the subject of your attraction
tugging at you? Or is it you — on your own volition — moved by your desire
to approach the subject?

The challenge posed by this question is introduced in the Hebrew Creation story when the first human couple ate of the Forbidden Fruit in the
Garden of Eden. Had they eaten of it because they were attracted to it, drawn
to it, found it overwhelmingly fascinating — it would not have been so
terribly wrong. The error, Judaism teaches, is that they ate of the Forbidden
Fruit not because they themselves desired to do so, but because they allowed
themselves to be *pulled* into it, to be *talked* into it.[4] In fact, the narrative in
the story tells us that they did not actually find the fruit attractive until *after*
they had been pulled-in by the serpent's talking them into it.[5] Their attraction
to the Forbidden Fruit, in other words, did not originate in *them*, but *outside*
of them.

When we participate in relationship, whether it be personal or communal, we are often challenged by this; especially the Child of the Moon of See'vahn. It is confusing. It is muddy, just like the meaning of the word See'vahn itself. It is confusing, because on the one hand we find ourselves drawn into the spirit of the community, for example, and on the other hand, it may not be what we really want, but rather we are being pulled into the frenzy of it, the excitement of it, the spin. So it is especially important for the See'vahn child to initially establish whether she is truly — deep inside — drawn to what it is that the subject of her attraction is offering, or whether she is actually being *pulled* by the subject of her attraction and therefore thrown into a dizzying spin that makes it feel as *if* she has found what she longs for.

The tribe associated with See'vahn, לוי Ley'vee, is so named because his mother, Ley'ah, still competing for the love of Jacob, gets the sense that her husband is now going to feel closer to her since she's given birth to their three sons. And so she calls this one Ley'vee, from the word *lavah* לוה, which means "connected" — as in "Now my husband will connect himself to me."[6]

Ley'vee grows up very bonded with his brother Shim'on. They are grouped together in the story, and are specifically referred to as Brothers, as in "Shim'on and Ley'vee are brothers"[7] — separate from their ten other brothers. Together, they posed a great danger, both being overly zealous. The difference in their zeal is that Ley'vee is zealous on behalf of spirit and Shim'on is zealous on behalf of body. The two joined forces in wiping out the male inhabitants of Sh'chem after their sister was taken by the *prince* of Sh'chem — Shim'on because his sister had been physically abused, and Ley'vee because his sister had been spiritually abused. These distinctions become more obvious later in the incident that occurred in the desert with Shim'on. When a descendant of Shim'on, Zimri, spitefully had sex with a Midianite woman, Koz'bee, in front of Moses' tent, it was a descendant of Ley'vee, Pin'chas, who reacted by running his spear through them both.[8] One acted with overzealousness in defiant demonstration of the sensuous, and the other acted with overzealousness in defiant demonstration of the spiritual. Ironically, Moses, himself of the tribe of Ley'vee, did not react at all to the disrespectful spectacle. The Kabbalah tells us that he saw beyond the brazenness of Zimri's action; he saw that actually Zimri and Koz'bee *belonged* together, only not right in that moment, and not in that particular context.[9] And so he froze, not knowing what to do, or if he ought to do anything about it, altogether. Moses then becomes the quieting factor of Ley'vee, along with his brother Aaron whose descendants inherit the priesthood, devoting their zeal to spirit, to worship.

Just as the zealous tribe of Shim'on is not designated leadership among the tribes of Israel whatsoever, the zealous tribe of Ley'vee is not apportioned any land of their own but are spread across the rest of the tribal communities as ritual facilitators. [10] The two are kept out of trouble, their zeal redirected where it cannot do any harm, only good.

Ley'vee is the ancestor of Miriam, Aaron, and Moses, [11] which also means he was the ancestor of (1) the leadership that redeemed our people from bondage in Egypt, (2) the leadership that guided them across their 40-year trek through the desert, (3) the leadership that transmitted the Torah and its details to the people, (4) the leadership that nurtured the people for 40 years with water and food, (5) the leadership responsible for transporting and maintaining the Sacred Ark of the Covenant during the desert journey, and (6) the leadership of the altar rituals through what became known as the כהנים *ko'hanim* and the לוים *Leh'vee'yeem,* the Priests and the Levites. All of these important components of Redemption, Revelation, and Worship, originated from the tribe of Ley'vee.

The three redeemers, Miriam, Aaron and Moses, [12] correspond in turn to the three Mothers of Creation mentioned in the ancient Kabbalah: Air, Water, Fire. אויר מים אש *Ah'veer, Mah'yeem, Esh.* [13] Moses, who nurtured the people through speech by teaching the Torah, corresponds to Air, or Breath, and represents Revelation. Miriam, in whose merit the people had water in the desert, [14] corresponds to Water, and represents Redemption because she is the one who first opened the people's hearts to the possibility of redemption by successfully talking them out of their resolve to abstain from intimacy during their enslavement [15] — which would have eventually rendered them extinct. "It is in the merit of the righteous women of Israel," the ancient rabbis taught, "that our ancestors were redeemed from Egypt." [16] Aaron, who facilitated the rites of the burnt offerings, corresponds to Fire, and therefore represents Worship.

The Totem for the tribe of Ley'vee לוי is the mysterious ancient oracle of the early Hebrews — the אורים ותמים *urim v'tumim* — literally: "Illuminations and Clarifications," as this oracle was consulted when things were muddy, confusing, unclear to the nation as to what to do, how to deal with an issue of tribal, individual or inter-tribal concern. This elusive oracle was concealed within the breastplate of the High Priest, who would meditate on the question brought to him, and his heart would receive the transmission from the oracle within the breastplate that hung over his heart. They say that the letters of the tribal names inscribed on the stones of the breastplate would actually light up in a cryptic sequence that would convey a coded message. [17] The breastplate, in turn, was a ceremonial garment that had twelve sacred stones sewn onto it, each representative of one of the twelve tribes. [18] The fact that the oracle of clarification was sewn into the breastplate, meaning that it rested against the heart, teaches us how important heart is in our search for clarity. We need to think and reason, yet we need also to pay attention to what we are *feeling* about any given situation. When we wish to listen to our Self, to hear what we are truly feeling deep inside, we are taught to go to the heart, because, as the Zohar puts it: שמיעה תליא בלבא *sh'mee'ya tol'yeh beh'lee'ba* — "Listening depends upon the heart."[19]

And indeed, the Levites represented the heart of the nation. During the 40-year desert journey, they were positioned in the center of the tribal configuration. They tended to, carried and flanked the Holy Ark of the Covenant, the centerpiece of the nation.[20] They were the heart, the nucleus, of the people, and carried the Sacred Space of the Divine Presence, the cosmic energy that was the heart, the pulse, of the community, sending the warmth of the Life Flow through the veins of the nation. No one does this better than the carrier of the tension between the opposites, the Gemini, the quality of Ley'vee.

The stone for the tribe of Ley'vee, and therefore for the Moon of See'vahn, is the Emerald ברקת *bo'reket,* whose quality is refraction of Divine light which has to do with filtering and directing the primeval Light of Creation, the Divine Light, as it radiates into the Created World, directing that Light and redirecting that Light where it is needed most for restoration, for healing, for empowering, for energizing. The role of the Levites at the altar space was primarily to facilitate chant and provide music during the ceremonies while the Ko'haneem performed their rituals for the public.

Emerald also melts down what is stoic, what is stuck, and rekindles the flames of passion and emotion where either has frozen or been blocked. Like Miriam did in Egypt for the people. Emerald opens up the heart, creates an inviting atmosphere or sensation in which one can feel safe and comfortable enough to emote, to feel, as it unblocks the impediments to the flow of our aliveness. This is what the Levites were assigned to do at the Sacred Altar in ancient Israel. Their role was to sing, to bring music to the temple rites. And when a person approached the altar to offer a sacrifice for some wrongdoing in their life, it was the Levite's job to bring song and chant to the ritual so that the person bringing the offering would be helped out of their solemnity, out of their depression and heaviness of guilt. After all, it is written: "Serve God with joy; come before God with song."[21] The Zohar, commenting on that verse in Psalms, asks: "How can someone bringing an offering to atone for their wrongdoing be expected to do this service in joy and song? On the contrary, would they not most likely be approaching the Sacred Altar despondent and with a heavy heart? Thus it was the role of the Levite to chant during the ritual in order to bring the comforting power of music to the person, and the role of the Ko'hayn to bring joy to the person by performing the rite with a countenance of joy."[22]

The emerald is therefore in its own right, by itself, a very sacred stone in that it incorporates both the joy of the Ko'hayn and the comforting chant of the Levite, both of which were intended to soften the rigidity of solemnity, sadness, and depression, due to the weightiness of guilt, through celebrative song and joyful countenance.

The emerald is the keeper of the many seemingly opposing forces that filter simultaneously through the primeval Light of Creation. It tempers the extremes, by virtue of being able to hold all extremes, all opposite forces, in balance. Each of the twelve tribes of Israel had totally differing customs and perspectives gained from differing interpretations of the revelation at Sinai, of the Torah. Yet they were unified as one nation, one people, by virtue of each tribe having its own representative of the tribe of Ley'vee, the tribe of the Emerald stone, keepers of diversity, and thereby unifying forces of conflicting pathways. They were not tied to any specifics, not to any specific territory, any particular definition or role. Their Totem was colorless, crystal clear, capable of reflecting all colors, not a specific one alone.

No wonder the herb of the sacred incense offering that corresponds to the tribe of Ley'vee, is Galbanum, or חלבונה *chal'vo'nah*, which etymologically translates as "applied understanding" as well as "applied whiteness" (חל *Chahl* = to apply; לבן *Lah'vahn* = white; בינה *Vee'nah* = understanding). It is the gift of the See'vahn person, the gift of the tribal quality of Ley'vee, to apply, to manifest, all the possibilities, all the variables, toward the achievement of clarity. White light has all the colors in a state of potential. The child of See'vahn is gifted with juggling the variables of different angles and vantage points in such a way as to bring forth each their merit, their particular color, their particular quality, so that the gift of each is more pronounced and acknowledged than the conflict that sizzles in the chasms that separate them. To do so requires the application of both, Understanding, and the mystique of the White Light. One can go through life filled with gifts and qualities that are amazing, yet without applying them in ways that those gifts can both, enrich the quality of one's own life walk and enrich the quality of the life walk of others. One can amass bricks and steel beams to build a house, but nothing happens with just having the supplies on hand; it all waits for application, translation into Being.

This herb is helpful in moving us out of stuck places toward action, toward application, toward building upon the learning we know, or the gifts we possess. In the mix of the sacred incense, this herb sought out the individual attributes of each of the other herbs and enabled their application to the mixture and to the intention of the offering, which varied according to the situation and need of the people.

The House of the Moon of See'vahn, it is בית האחים *Bayt Ha'Ah'cheem* the House of Fellowship. This is connected to the quality of attraction, since it is attraction that brings people together in fellowship. And again, the challenge is to make sure the connection to community or to people or things originates in your soul of souls and is not a result of being pulled into, talked into or spun into connection. Otherwise, the fellowship becomes anything but that. Often we are pulled in by something or someone by virtue of our fascination with them, something within them that draws us like a magnet. It is then that we need to also look inside, listen to our heart, to see whether we too desire the connection.

The Shadow Moon for See'vahn is the month of כסלו Kees'lev, which literally translates as "Basket of the Heart," literally a containment for the heart. The attraction of Heart to a child of Muddiness, a child of See'vahn, is understandably great. Because while mud, Earth and water, opens the seed of potential to the horizon of possibility, Heart is that possibility already pumping in full force, fruition in its potent and ripe state. In *See'vahn*, for example, the Torah was given, and in its shadow month *Kees'lev* the *mish'kahn* משכן, the sacred space of the Holy Ark of the Covenant, was completed and set up. In See'vahn the Torah was *born*; in Kees'lev, it manifested, it came to fruition. Sometimes *instant* is more attractive than process. The House for the Shadow Moon of See'vahn — Kees'lev — is *Bayt Ha'd'rah'cheem* בית הדרכים, House of Many Pathways, many opportunities. We are taught by our ancestors that it matters not so much which roads we choose to take or end up taking in our lives, as much as it matters how we choose to *journey* along those pathways. The House of Many Pathways is often a challenge for the See'vahn child since See'vahn's quality of Attraction can lead the See'vahn child to become seduced by the attraction of not one or two but "Many Pathways," the quality of its shadow moon. The seductive qualities of this Shadow Moon for the See'vahn child is quite strong.

The Zodiac for See'vahn, according to our Moon Wheel, is תאומים — *T'oo'meem*, "Twins," or in other languages "Gemini." Inherent within the characteristic of the Moon of Twins is the inclination toward seeing double, meaning seeing the same thing from differing, and often opposing, vantage points. Just like the double meaning we just discussed around See'vahn's quality, Attraction — as in being drawn *to*, or being pulled *by*, the attraction. Again, we need to go back to the Totem associated with the tribe of See'vahnh, the Oracle of Clarity, the oracle that sits over our hearts. It is about the challenge of Revelation, since Revelation occurred in this month at Mount Sinai about 3,300 years ago. And Revelation is filled with a variety of perspectives around its interpretation: Muddy.

The Gemini quality in the tribe of Ley'vee was its containment of very opposite qualities: compassion and sternness. Levites like Aaron were known for their deep compassion and love for the people even when the people erred.[23] Levites like Aaron's grandson Pin'chas were known for their intolerance and zealousness and therefore also their harsh reaction to the people when there was dissent.[24] Moses and Miriam both shared a balance of both traits. On the one hand, because of Miriam's compassion, she spoke on behalf of her sister-in-law Tzee'po'rah — Moses' wife — when she noticed Moses was avoiding intimacy with her.[25] On the other hand, in her zeal she acted harshly in critiquing Moses for it behind his back instead of talking to Moses directly about it. Moses, too, exhibited throughout the story deep compassion for the people. He pleaded on their behalf when they erred and was ready to give up his life for them.[26] He also exhibited zealous reactions to the people's rebelliousness that were at times excessively harsh.[27]

The letter associated with See'vahn is the *za'yeen* ז, which literally translates as "Weapon." Weapon implies overriding other, whether with a knife, a sword, a bullet, or a baseball bat. All of them touch and invade or enter the Other in a damaging or a destructive way when we use them. However, Weapon is also about defense. So, it too, is a double-edged sword, excuse the pun. It can be destructive, yes, and it can also salvage one's own well-being or that of another. We can use this quality for purposes of utter destruction where the damage is intended for the sole purpose of destroying another, or we can use this quality for purposes of defense, where there is damage, but the intended purpose is preservation of self or other. Ironically, the word *za'yeen* is also related to the ancient Hebrew word for "provide" or "nurture," as in *zohn* זן. We can channel our zeal in life either way. It is our choice.

NOTES

1. Genesis 1:2.
2. *Midrash Tanchuma, Yit'ro*, No. 13.
3. 2nd century Rabbi Yannai in *Talmud Yerushalmi, Sandedrin* 4:2.
4. 19th-century Rabbi Yoizel Horovitz in *Mahd'rey'gaht Ha'Adam*.
5. Genesis 3:6.
6. Genesis 29:34.
7. Genesis 49:5.
8. Numbers 25:7-8.
9. 16th-century Rabbi Yitzchak Luria, quoted in *Mey Ha'Shee'lo'ach*, Vol. 1, *Parashat Pinchas — "Va'yar Pinchas"*.
10. Numbers 18:24.
11. Numbers 26:59.
12. Micah 6:4 and *Midrash Vayik'ra Rabbah* 27:6.
13. *Sefer Yetzirah* 3:1.
14. *Midrash Bamid'bar Rabbah* 1:2.
15. *Midrash Pesik'ta Rabbatee* 43:4.
16. *Midrash Bamid'bar Rabbah* 3:6.
17. *Talmud Bav'li, Yoma* 73b.
18. Exodus 28:17-21.
19. *Tikunei Zohar* [*Tikuna* 58], folio 92a.
20. Numbers 2:17, 3:25 and 10:17.
21. Psalms 100:2.
22. Zohar, vol. 3, folio 8a.
23. *Talmud Bav'li, Sanhedrin* 6b; *Midrash Pirkei D'Rebbe Eliezer*, Ch. 17.
24. Exodus 32:25-28 and Numbers 25:7-8.
25. Numbers 12:1.
26. Exodus 32:32.
27. Exodus 32:25-28 and Numbers 20:10.

Chapter Five

Tamuz

(June 9-August 6)

Tamuz תמוז, meaning "Completeness of Strength"

Attribute: Vision ראיה *r'eeyah*

Tribe: Ye'hudah יהודה meaning "Gratitude to God"

Tribal Totem: Lion אריה *ahr'yeh* whose quality is Warrior

Tribal Stone: Turquoise נפך *no'pech* whose quality is Power and Victory in Struggle

Tribal Herb: Frankincense לבונה *l'vo'nah*

House: Ancestors בית האבות *bayt ha'a'vo't*

Zodiac: Crab סרטן *sar'tahn*

Letter: *chet.* ח Fence

Tribal Flag: כחול *keh'cho'l*, Sky Blue with the image of a lion

Tribal Direction: East, קדם *kedem*, "Beginning," and מזרח *meez'rach*, "Shining"

תמוז *Tamuz* translates as Completeness of Strength, or Completely Adamant (תם *tahm*: complete; עוז: strength or tenacity), as in unwavering in one's power and fortitude. *Tam* also translates as Simple, as in innocently meandering through life, sitting back and allowing life to go on without much of our participation. Simplicity as incidental. *Uz* or *oz*, also translates as "stubborn." It is also the month when the Great Flood in Noah's time began to subside, and the tops of the highest mountains first became visible. [1]

This is a month that commemorates the beginning of the end, the fateful assault on Jerusalem by the Babylonians that eventually brought down the First Temple, exiled our prophets and many of our tribes, and destroyed the

First Jewish Commonwealth about 2,600 years ago. It is also believed to be the beginning of the siege around Jerusalem 500 years later that led to the destruction of the *Second* Temple and the Second Jewish Commonwealth — this time by the Romans. These chains of events began on the 17th of the Moon of Tamuz.[2] In other words, they occurred after the moon had reached its fullness and had begun to wane. Strength and tenaciousness certainly brings one closer to completeness, to accomplishment, but the lesson of Tamuz is about maintaining consistency, not allowing the power we have brought forth to relax, to wane, to slip away by stepping back from its continuance. When we sit back in the simple faith that we've done enough, put in enough effort, and our vision or goal will now take on a life of its own and continue to evolve — the walls around us begin to tumble and the invasion of failure and downfall meets us instead.

Likewise, as a people we grew too comfortable, became overly bureau-cratic, excessively structured with monarchs, temples, rote rituals, and our life force as a nation began to slowly ebb and lose its momentum. Our prophets cried to us in the streets, warning us, trying to wake us out of our slumber, but we paid them no mind. Everything was fine the way it was. Simplicity set in, naivety took us over and eventually callousness.[3] And there we remained with the same tenaciousness as that which had once given us the strength to become a nation of God Wrestlers — the very meaning of ישראל *yisra'el*.[4] And eventually, the outside world overtook us and carried us away in chains.[5]

The Moon of Tamuz is the beginning of the period during which the night begins to borrow from the day — darkness partakes of light, tragedy reaches into the coffers of hope and draws on faith.[6] As bleak as it is in times of heaviness, Tamuz teaches us to use the darkness to *discover* the light: "In the light," the ancient ones reminded us, "one cannot see what is in the darkness; in the darkness, however, one can see into the light."[7] If you are standing in the dark, you can easily see what is going on inside a home that is lit up, whereas if you were in a lit-up home looking out your window at night, you would not be able to see what is going on outside.

Tamuz is also the moon during which the Golden Calf was constructed and worshiped.[8] In other words, Tamuz, like its meaning, is a moon that exudes both, empowerment and simplicity, tenaciousness and completeness; we can choose to use our strength, our power, toward completeness, toward purpose, or we can use that tenacity to remain in a state of complacency. We can direct our powers toward building the Holy Temple and shattering the Golden Calf, or building the Golden Calf and shattering the Holy Temple.

Tamuz is when the Sun is at its hottest, the beginning of seasonal shifting from the place of balance. Prior to this moon, the days have been as long as the nights for a while, and it is not too hot, not too cold, it is all in balance. With the arrival of Tamuz, however, the heat intensifies, the days become longer than the nights. In other words, it is a time of shifting away from the place of Balance, which in turn can lead to havoc, confusion and vulnerability, both individually and collectively. [9]

The ancients reminded us, however, that in the very whirlwind of confusion and imbalance, we can discover the greatest gifts, and claim our highest powers, if we but push through the impediments. The eagle, Moses reminded us over 3,300 years ago, teaches its chicks to discover their own strength and capacity by stirring the nest so that they fall out. And while falling toward their possibly tragic deaths, they flap their wings desperately, and in their struggle discover that they can fly; in their greatest moment of vulnerability and weakness, they discover their power and independence. [10]

During Tamuz, the ancients taught, God calls out in a resounding, vibrational sound that is inaudible to mortals, a sound that summons the deepest recesses of our powers. This Divine call delivers courage to those parts of us that are afraid — even to those animals who live in fear of predators — a call for courage and stamina. [11] Like the 18th-century Rebbe Nachmon of Breslav taught: "Within the very obstacles that prevent you from discovering God, is precisely where God waits to be discovered." [12] Tamuz is then an incredible challenge, and equally an incredible opportunity.

The attribute of the Moon of Tamuz is ראיה *R'ee'yah* — Vision: to appreciate the gift of what comes to us, and not be intimidated by it. To become a true Judah-ite, we need clarity of vision, the capacity to see beyond the way in which we are *accustomed* to seeing — to see beyond what something appears to be, to look deeper into the literal experience to discover the mystery that it conceals. That way, we do not lose faith or hope in the face of that which seeks to intimidate us, to block us. We will then not fear the whirling swords of fire that the Cherubim wave in front of us as we strive to make our way back to the Tree of Life. [13] The word Cherub, or כרוב *k'ruv* in Hebrew, is rooted in the word for closeness קרוב *kee'ruv*, nearness, approachability. The very things that seem to keep us distant are the very things that at the same time beckon to us to dare approach. (Note: In the ancient midrashic tradition of creative interpretation, associations of meanings are freely made between words that sound the same even if their spelling differs.)

The tribal archetype of Tamuz is יהודה *Yehudah*, which means "Appreciating what God Brings Us" whether trials or gifts. This is the essence of the meaning behind Judah, or Judaism. It is about always being grateful even for what we don't yet understand — an appreciation born out of trust, faith. Judah's mother, לאה Ley'ah, is unhappy about her husband's lack of appreciation of her, his attention being mostly focused on her sister רחל Ra'chel. She names her *first* three sons based on her agony, but when she gives birth to her fourth son, Yehudah, she exclaims: "This time, I simply thank God." [14] She has pushed through the obstacles, claimed her own power, and discovered joy within *herself* as opposed to seeking it elsewhere or hoping it would come from someone else.

Yehudah is not only elected to lead his brothers, including the three that are older than him, he is also designated as the ancestral lineage carrier of the Messiah.[15] He is fierce like a lion, yet humble in his demeanor. When he errs, he is not afraid of openly admitting his guilt,[16] a trait that trickles down through the ages to his descendant David, who confesses and owns responsibility for his illicit union with Bathsheba and his involvement in the demise of her husband Uriah.[17] Yehudah, then, is an archetype that combines ferocity, honesty, and humility.

The Totem of the tribe of Judah, and the Moon of Tamuz, is Lion אריה *ahr'yeh* whose quality is Warrior, with the wisdom to know when to use one's full power and when to hold back from using one's full power. The lion, like the Divine light, walks in balance between the extremes, between fierceness and being overpowering. This is why in Hebrew we call Lion *ahr'yeh*, which is two words אור *ohr* and יה *yah* — Light and God, or the God Light. The God Light, like the lion, is both fierce and overpowering, as well as healing and nurturing, depending on what is called for in the circumstance and the moment. The lion is also the sacred keeper of the East, place of new beginnings, the very same direction whose charge was assigned to the tribe of Judah during the desert journey.[18] East in Hebrew is מזרח *meez'rach*, which implies "Shining," as East is where Sun begins to shine across the planet, and קדם *kedem*, which implies "Beginning." New beginnings always require us to bring forth our deepest warrior self. New beginnings are often intimidating, scary, exciting, fun, all at the same time.

The lion is also patient and playful, frolicking with young cubs and enduring patiently their playful swipes and climbing. But when threatened, or needing to hunt prey to sustain the family, the lion shifts to become the warrior. The true warrior is the one who is bold and fierce in the battlefield and a gentle kitten at home.

The Stone associated with Tamuz and the tribe of Judah, is נופך *no'pehch* — Turquoise, whose quality is Strength and Victory in times of struggle, related to the word פח *pahch*, which means a burning ember. It is about endurance, keeping the inner fire burning, the passion to overcome, to see things through to its climax, to its ultimate realization.

The Herb associated with Tamuz is Frankincense לבונה *l'vo'nah*, which is about everything in its original state of potentiality. It is the dream before it is realized. It is all the colors before they are manifested, before they are individuated. It is like the ray of Sun that is light white color which is then translated by the mist of rainfall into many *different* colors, individuated. Frankincense reminds us that everything is One, but not the same. It carries the power of individuation, of bringing forth the unity of diversity and the diverseness of unity. In the blend of the sacred incense offering, it is the blending element, magically blending all the qualities of all the other plants into a singular mix where a single aroma is created, a single stream of smoke, yet without overriding the individual quality of each plant. Paradoxical, or magical? Or, both?

The House associated with Tamuz is בית האבות *Bait Ha'A'vo't* — House of Ancestors. To live in the House of Ancestors demands of us that we rise to the occasion of becoming ancestors *ourselves*, not only living in the shadows of those who came *before* us, but also becoming the shadows for those who will come after us.

Living in the House of Ancestors requires us to take stock of our capabilities, not be overridden by our failures, but to focus on and build upon our achievements, our talents, our unique selves. All of our ancestors, the Torah shows us, had their moments of failure, of falling, but never did they allow those failings to stop them dead in their tracks. They moved on, they moved through it all, and thereby became ancestors, models, exemplifying to us how to walk through blizzards, traverse storms, and rise up like the Phoenix from out of the ashes, again and again.

The Shadow Moon for Tamuz is Tey'veht טבת, whose house is *Bay't Ha'Mal'chut* בית המלכות - House of Sovereignty, which is about control, wielding one's presence and power over others. This is the challenge to the visionary, to the Judah archetype, to the lion, the warrior - to know when to pull back so as not to overwhelm others with their power and clarity. Because, being a warrior means also to know when to be silent even when one has more clarity about a situation than others; to know when to step back and allow others to figure things out, make their mistakes, or, hopefully, shine, and discover their own powers and greatness.

The Zodiac quality of Tamuz is the סרטן *Sar'tan* — Crab. This is the drama of our emerging from Mother (water) to find our own balance, our own independence, our own selfhood. The crab moves from sea to land, from the womb of newness to the daring adventure of *engaging* newness, leaving the sea for dry land, and dry land for the sea, transitioning interchangeably from spirituality to physicality. The crab then reminds us of the oneness of both and the equal need and importance of both in our lives. Water represents spirituality, Earth represents physicality.

Crab teaches us the sanctity of merging the two realities into our everyday lives, spirit and matter, body and soul, and not to live exclusively in one or the other but in both at the same time. Judaism brings this important lesson home to us through our rituals, including our seasonal celebrations, all of which are spiritual in intention and physical in implementation. We celebrate Sukot, for example, with special sacred rites, but also with special feasting and physical joy, as is written in the Torah: "And you shall *rejoice* in your seasonal rites...and you shall be very happy." [19]

The Letter associated with Tamuz, is ח *Cheht* — Fence, boundary, the challenge of the visionary warrior, which is to maintain boundaries that keep us in balance as we walk the fine line between clarity and fogginess, certainty and doubt. What we vision for tomorrow is uncertain, it is but *vision*, not action. Whether it might *eventually* translate into action depends on whether we can create sufficient boundaries around it to maintain it, to trust in it, to not let it dissipate beyond our passion for it to happen; to not allow external voices to throw it off balance.

NOTES

1. Genesis 8:5.
2. *Mishnah, Ta'anit* 4:6.
3. E.g., Isaiah, Chapter 1 and 29:9-13 and Chapter 58; Jeremiah 5:12; Hosea 9:14.
4. Genesis 32:29.
5. Jeremiah, Chapter 39.
6. *Midrash Tanchuma, Mishpatim,* Ch. 15.
7. *Midrash Tanchuma, Tetzaveh,* Ch. 8.
8. *Midrash Pesik'ta D'Rav Kahana* 28:3.
9. 16th-century Rabbi Yehudah Loew of Prague [MaHaRaL] in *Netzach Yisroel*, Ch. 8, folio 58.
10. Deuteronomy 32:11.
11. *Otzar HaMidrashim, Hashem B'choch'mah Yasad Aretz, Keta* 6.
12. *Likutei MoHaRaN*, Ch. 115.
13. Genesis 3:24.
14. Genesis 29:35.
15. *Midrash Bereisheet Rabbah* 97:10.
16. Genesis 38:26.
17. Second Samuel 12:13.
18. Numbers 2:3.
19. Deuteronomy 16:14 and 15.

Chapter Six

Ahv

(July 8-September 5)

Ahv אב, meaning "Ancestor"

Attribute: Listening שמיעה *sh'mee'ah*

Tribe: Yee'sas'char יששכר meaning "shall recompense"

Tribal Totem: Donkey חמור *cha'mor* whose quality is Endurance

Tribal Stone: Sapphire ספיר *sah'peer* whose quality is Healing

Tribal Herb: Myrrh מור *mo'r*

House: Children בית הבנים *bayt ha'ba'neem*

Zodiac: Lion אריה *ar'yeh*

Letter: *tet* ט Snake

Tribal Flag: שחור דומה לכחול Bluish Black, *shachor do'meh le'ka'chol*, with image of the Sun and moon

Tribal Direction: East, קדם *kedem*, "Beginning," and מזרח *meez'rach*, "Shining"

אב *Ahv* is usually referred to as מנחם אב *Menachem Ahv*. Menachem means "will bring comfort." Ahv is the moon in which both our temples were destroyed, first by the Babylonians in 480 B.C.E., and again by the Romans in 68 C.E. In line with the Jewish people's tendency to look for the spark of good in all evil, purity in impurity, light in darkness, love in hate — it became our belief that the very month in which we lost our temples and were exiled, is the very month in which the Messiah will be born to redeem us from exile and bring us consolation.[1]

Ahv literally means "Ancestor." Or "head of" as in leadership. And while it is considered a tragic month because of what happened to our people during that time of the year, it is also the month in which our ancestors celebrated one of the most festive days on the Hebraic calendar: טו באב *Tu B'ahv*, or Fifteenth of Ahv.

The Talmud records how "Israel has never experienced days as festive and joyful as the Day of Atonement, Yom Kippur, and the fifteenth day of the moon of Ahv. What happened on those days? "The women would dress in white garments, borrowed from one another [so that no one would know the social status of the other], and dance in the vineyards."[2] For Yom Kippur it was a dance of celebration that our wrongdoings were forgiven and we can now start anew. For the 15th of Ahv it was the beginning of the season of withdrawal from extreme, when the blazing heat of the desert Sun began to slowly dissipate, allowing the foliage to breathe once more and for the clouds to form and bring the rains. Ahv is therefore a very full month, a month filled with all of what life bring us, sadness, joy, tragedy, celebration, hopelessness, and redemption. As such, it is the *ancestor* moon, the head of, the umbrella, so to speak, of all the various ways in which we are birthed and re-birthed, and in which we are challenged and realized.

The attribute associated with Ahv is שמיעה *sh'mee'ah*, which means Listening. Listening is an intake of encounters that is more focused than simply "hearing." The Ahv child takes in deeply and intensely what they experience. Just as ancestor implies also the template of future, so does the Ahv child, the ancestor child, form templates for future from everything they encounter. It does not go in one ear and out the other, as they say. It sticks and it builds one experience atop the other, becoming often a weighty load to carry. Few can carry such weight and endure the heaviness of it as the child of Ahv, the ancestor moon person upon whose shoulders so many others find their footing.

This moon corresponds to the tribe of יששכר Yee'sas'char. The tribe of Yee'sas'char is described as gifted with the intuitive capacity to know things ahead of time. The other tribes would therefore seek their counsel concerning the future. In the Tenach (the Hebrew Scriptures) they are described as "Knowers of the Understanding of Times."[3] Even the Totem of Yee'sas'char, the donkey, determines times when it will walk, times it will not be budged. This tribe, this moon, this Totem, is about mastering time as opposed to allowing oneself to be mastered by time. We are often driven by time-bound circumstances and responsibilities. The Ahv child is a Knower of Times, who dances in synch with the force we call time, with the movement and cadence of the ever-unfolding phases of time. The child of Ahv freezes time, collects every moment, and engages it in real-time relationship. Yee'sas'char was positioned in the East during the 40-year desert trek, place of new beginnings.[4] East in Hebrew is מזרח *meez'rach*, which implies "Shining," as East is where Sun reveals itself at day break, and קדם *kedem*, which implies "Beginning." As Keepers of Time, East was a fitting direction to be placed in their charge, since East is where Sun emerges and determines time for the ensuing day.

The child of Ahv, remember, is a listener, a deep deep listener, capturing every situation of every moment, and shouldering the ever-growing weight of time and both its gifts and challenges. Time is also described in the very beginning of the ancient mystical Scroll of Creation[5] as the mediating force between the absolute, non-negotiable laws of the universe on one hand, and the more fluid and unpredictable force of individual human unfolding through free will choices and action on the other hand. The Ahv child is therefore a juggler of the practical and the dream, of what is and what *can* be, as in Ahv being the moon in which our people's commonwealth was *shattered*, and also the moon in which we dream about our restoration and redemption.

The word *Yee'sas'char* stems from the Hebrew term for wages, or hiring, and he was so named by his mother Ley'ah because he was conceived the night she "hired" Jacob to make love to her. It had actually been Rachel's night to be with Jacob, but at Ley'ah's request, Rachel had agreed to allow Ley'ah to be with him for the night in exchange for some nice ripe mandrakes that Ley'ah's son Reuvayn had plucked that day.[6] (According to the 11th-century Rabbi Shmuel ben Meir, it was a fig). Note how Reuvayn once again interferes in his father's love life. As mentioned in an earlier chapter, he had made love to Bil'hah, one of his father's half-wives[7] . It is also interesting that Ley'ah does not intend Yee'sas'char's name to represent the bartering she did with her sister the night he was conceived. Rather, she sees his birth as God compensating her, rewarding her — that is — because earlier she had allowed her helper-companion Zil'pah to make love with Jacob for the purpose of bearing more children. Rachel had done the same, having Jacob make love with her helper-companion Bil'hah to bear children on *her* behalf since she was infertile for a while. But for Ley'ah, such an act was even more precious because it was hard enough for her to share her husband with her sister whom he loved more than her, let alone also share her husband with Zil'pah. She thereby intensified her endurance for the sake of forging future generations. Born of this intent is Yee'sas'char, whose archetype is endurance and foresight.

The Totem for Yee'sas'char and the month of Ahv is the Donkey, חמור *cha'mor* — whose quality is Endurance, carrying other people's burdens yet maintaining its own sense of selfhood. While the donkey endures whatever we might choose to burden it with, nevertheless it also has a mind of its own and will walk or not walk, move or not move, depending on whether it feels it is the right time or not. Donkey also represents, in the animal world at least, the most dense realm of matter, physical matter in its most fully manifested form, which is why, in Hebrew, the donkey is called *cha'mor*, from the word חומר *cho'mer*, which means simply Matter.[8] Its unusual capacity, no matter its size, to carry, to hold what is placed on it, equates it to the essential meaning of matter in the Judaic mindset, which is about holding and carrying the manifestation of the Creator's dream of Creation. Yet, while the Ahv child carries a lot in their life walk, they are also richly rewarded, as is the meaning of the name for the tribe of Ahv, *Yee'sas'char* — literally: "shall recompense"[9] — related to the theme of the month of Ahv itself, exile and redemption, sadness and dance. The power of Donkey for the child of Ahv is not only about enduring the weightiness of life circumstances but also maintaining a staunch, tenacious stand in life, a power of standing one's ground and weathering all storms, no matter how severe.

Throughout the entire Sacred Scriptures of the Hebrews, only two animals are described as being capable of human speech: Snake and Donkey. Snake talks the first humans into eating of the Tree of Knowledge and Donkey talks the Midianite prophet Bil'ahm out of striking him when he is blocked along the way by an angel. Bil'ahm had been hired by the Moabites to destroy the Israelites with his curses. He saddles his donkey and rides out to do just that when God sends an angel to block him. Even though he is a prophet, Bil'ahm is unable to see the angel, whereas his donkey does see the angel and therefore refuses to budge. Bil'ahm then begins beating his donkey, trying to make him move, but to no avail. Finally, God "opens the mouth of the donkey"[10] — meaning, enables the donkey to speak — at which point the donkey voices her protest over the beatings:

> Donkey: "What have I ever done to you that you should strike me these three times?"
> Bil'ahm: "Because you have revolted against me. Were I in possession of a sword in my hand, I would kill you right here and now!"
> Donkey: "Am I not your loyal donkey upon whom you have ridden from before you even existed, all the way to this day? Would I ever have cause to endanger myself by doing what you accuse me of?"
> Bil'ahm: "No."

God then "opens the eyes of Bil'ahm" — meaning, enables Bil'ahm to see what the donkey sees: an angel standing in their path with sword drawn.[11]

In the oral tradition, this biblical story is embellished further:[12]

> Donkey: "What have I ever done to you that you should strike me these three times?"
> Bil'ahm: "Because you have revolted against me. Were I in possession of a sword in my hand, I would kill you right here and now!"
> Donkey: "Me, you can't kill unless you have a sword in your hand? Well, then, how do you propose to destroy an entire nation with just your tongue?"
> Bil'ahm was silent. He could find no retort.

The oral tradition also teaches us that among very special phenomena that God created at the twilight of the Sixth Cycle of Creation was "the mouth of the donkey," meaning Bil'ahm's donkey's capacity for speech in that moment.[13] The second-century Rabbi Shim'on bar Yo'chai elaborates on this teaching and explains that the term "mouth of the donkey" refers to a deeply mystical concept, that at the beginning of time in the process of Genesis, Creator concealed the power of the Feminine — which is Timing of Expression and Fruition - deep within the Great Void. There, like seed within womb, this force waits for the right timing before emerging to coincide with the need for it within the Created Universe, the manifestation of which is embodied by the angelic being known as קמריאל Kam'ree'el. And so, when the Torah recounts how God "opened the mouth of the donkey" in the story of Bil'ahm, it means that God opened the mouth of the Great Void to conjure forth the concealed force of the Feminine, which in this particular instance became the then timely need for the specific power of expression, of communication. This power was then integrated within the donkey by the angel Kam'ree'el, enabling the donkey to speak.[14] Once again, we have the theme of "timing," corresponding to the quality of the tribe known foremost for their acute awareness of timing.[15]

The donkey is a sacred animal in Judaism. The Hebrew ancestral prophets consistently chose donkeys over horses for their journeys, and obviously so did non-Jewish prophets like Bil'ahm. Sure-footed, powerful, and slow, the donkey helped to make sure the prophets were not just "seeing things" in the heat of their visioning but had sufficient time to "cool down" from ecstatic communion with the Divine to ascertain the clarity of their experiences. In a powerful vision, for example, Abraham is told to head to Mount Moriah and offer up his son Isaac to God. Had he jumped on a horse, he would have carried out the sacrifice within the day. Instead, "he saddled his donkey" and journeyed for three days,[16] enough time to "come down" from his prophetic visionary experience and get some clarity on the issue, so that his response is not in the heat of the moment but with authenticity. Even the bearer of the Messianic era is destined to arrive mounted on a donkey, slowly meandering into the turmoil of a world urgently needing redemption,[17] and doing so at the right time; not sooner, not later.

The narrative in the Torah about Abraham's journey to Moriah is puzzling. Once he and Isaac arrive at the foot of the mountain, he tells the two youths who accompanied them to "remain here with the donkey."[18] Why does the Torah narrative deem it so important to mention the donkey again? Would it not suffice to have Abraham instruct them to simply just *wait* there? What is "*with* the donkey" all about? But as mentioned earlier, the word for donkey, חמור *cha'mor*, implies elemental matter, or *cho'mer*, חומר , and in order to climb the mountain of Divine revelation, which is what the word *moree'yah* מוריה (Moriah) actually implies, one needs to separate oneself from one's *cho'mer* and reach beyond the limitations of the physical. Separating from one's *cho'mer* requires moving oneself beyond one's body self (the donkey) as well as one's emotive and cognitive selves (the two youths). This story is then also a metaphor for the journey of the soul toward Enlightenment.[19] The soul manifests herself in the persona in five ways: appetitive (נפש *nefesh* = donkey), emotive (רוח ru'ach = first youth), cognitive (נשמה *neshamah* = second youth), consciousness (חיה *chayyah* = Isaac), and uniqueness (יחידה *ye'chee'dah* = Abraham). Yet, everything rides on the donkey, the carrier, the vehicle, so to speak, who sets the pace of our life walk and carries us toward our destiny, toward the mountain that God shall show us[20] — all in good time.

The stone of the tribe of *Yee'sas'char* that was sewn into the breastplate of the ancient high priest of our people is none other than the most sacred of all stones: the Sapphire stone, the ספיר *sah'peer*, whose quality is about healing, and after which the Kabbalistic "Sephirot" are named.[21] *Sah'peer* also translates as "Telling," since this stone, as well as the *Sephirot*, "tell" of the Glory of God.[22] The sapphire is also the image the elders of Israel witnessed as they waited at the base of Mount Sinai and looked up at the mountain's glowing peak: "And they saw what seemed like the image of the glow of sapphire."[23]

Why is such a sacred and powerful and mystical stone as the sapphire stone assigned to the little-known tribe of *Yee'sas'char*? Because, the one who carries the most is the one who shines the most. As the Zohar puts it: "There is no light as brilliant as that light which emerges from out of the darkness."[24]

The herb for the moon of Ahv that was applied to the sacred incense offering at the ancient Hebrew altar, is Myrrh, מור *mo'r* in Hebrew, whose quality is about המתקה *hahm'takah*, or Sweetness. Literally, the Hebrew word *mo'r* is related at its root to the Hebrew word for Bitterness. Again we have the bitterness and sweetness quality of the moon of Ahv in its corresponding sacred herb. This herb is about the camouflage of mystery, the rose among the thorns, the flesh fruit within the harsh peel, the edible nut within the impregnable shell, the juicy treat within the spiky cacti, and so on. Myrrh contrasts its opposite, like darkness contrasts light and vice-versa, its presence calling forth its opposite by default. Whatever sweetness in flavor and in fragrance that may lie deep within the other herbs of the sacred incense blend, is brought forward, made loud, made to shout, made more vivid, more dramatic, more present, by the ingredient of Myrrh. It is a good herb to use, especially its smoke or its oils, when one is having trouble coming out of a dark place, a depressed state, a place of hopelessness in which one is struggling to discover any semblance of sweetness, of hope, of joy. Likewise, the child of Ahv is gifted with this capacity, this gift of soothing, restoring joy and healing to others, as well as the gift of calling forth in others *their* sweetness, *their* goodness, *their* strengths.

The House realm for the moon of Ahv is therefore *bayt ha'ba'neem* בית הבנים, the House of Children, since this quality is exactly what children need from their parents, the qualities of wisdom and stamina, and the gift of knowing how to build up another person, to restore them to their selfhood, to mirror to them their deepest gift of self — a skill inherent in the ancestor, and in the child of the Moon of Ancestor. The House of Children implies not only that the Ahv child makes for a wonderful parent; it also implies that the Ahv child retains even throughout their adulthood child-like qualities and vulner- abilities and are very sensitive because of their child-like open-heartedness, and are therefore often hurt easily due to their child-like trust and their faith in others.

The Shadow Moon of the month of Ahv — the one directly opposite Ahv on the ancient Kabbalistic wheel of astrological wisdom — is the month of Sh'vaht שבט, whose House is the House of Love, or *Bayt Ha'Ahavah* בית האהבה.

What is so shadowy about love for Ahv's House of Children?

When the Ahv child loves, the love is as deep as that of a parent to a child, and often this love spills into adult relationships which on the one hand gives the Ahv child the empowerment and stamina of Donkey to remain connected in a relationship no matter what, even if it hurts, which is not always healthy, and on the other hand, at times such tenacious commitment leads to a *deepening* of the relationship and a tempering of a quality of love gone wrong so that it turns right. Not many people have the patience and stamina as does the Ahv child, to stay solid and continue to love in spite of betrayal or hurt. This can of course *harm* the Ahv child if no change occurs in the situation and that very noble tendency to love no matter what — as a parent does a child — can eventually destroy the Ahv child. Therefore does the Torah warn against plowing your field with a donkey and a buffalo under the same yoke since the two have very different temperaments. [25]

The Totem of Ahv is the donkey; the Totem of its shadow moon Sh'vaht is the buffalo! As each of these two animals have a very different nature and pace of movement, so does the child of Ahv and the child of Sh'vaht each have a very distinct pace of seeing and understanding, and it often takes the buffalo time to catch up with the donkey's speed, and it takes time for the donkey to keep up with the ox's broader gait. [26] But the donkey's patience and its capacity to endure, enables the Ahv child to wait just a wee bit longer than most to see if the Sh'vaht partner can begin to see and understand what the Ahv child sees and understands. There are times, in other words, that the Ahv tendency ultimately wins over the Sh'vaht tendency and directs it to- ward the vision and truth of the Ahv child, in which case what could have been a *shadow* effect of love becomes in such instances an enriching and elevating and *ecstatic* effect of love.

The Shadow Moon for Ahv, however, also correlates to the Totem of the Wild Donkey, which is far more compatible than Buffalo, yet being wild it has no tolerance for being saddled and resists carrying any load. At times, the Ahv child might shirk off responsibility and refuse to endure one more ounce of issues to deal with, instead tempted to run off alongside the Wild Donkey of Sh'vaht. Everyone needs a break at some point, regardless of their capacity to carry the ever-intensifying weightiness of life's unrelenting challenges. Yet, there is a difference between taking a break from the demands and responsibilities of our lives, and fleeing from them altogether.

The Zodiac or מזל *mazal* for the moon of Ahv is the Lion, אריה *ar'yeh*, whose quality is Warrior. The warrior is endowed with the wisdom to know when to use her full power and when to hold back from using her full power. The lion, for example, does not go after animals just for the sake of killing, only when hungry or in self-defense. Likewise, the warrior is non-threatening, and only brings her power to the forefront when needed. The warrior knows her strength but doesn't flaunt it, yet when needed is the first one to step forward, to step up to the occasion. The lion is also the sacred keeper of the East, place of new beginnings. [27] New beginnings always require us to bring forth our deepest warrior self. The lion, like the Divine Light, walks in balance between the extremes, between fierceness and being overpowering; between patience and playfulness, frolicking with young cubs and enduring patiently their playful swipes and climbing. But when threatened, the lion shifts to become the warrior. The true warrior is the one who is bold and fierce in the battlefield and a gentle kitten at home. This is why in Hebrew we call Lion *ahr'yeh*, which is two words אור *ohr* and יה *yah* — Light and God, or the God Light, which, like the lion, is both fierce and overpowering, healing and nurturing, depending on what is called for in the circumstance and the moment.

The Hebrew letter or *o't* אות associated with the moon of Ahv is the letter ט *tet*, which implies Snake, and is actually shaped like a coiled snake ready to strike. Snake in Hebrew is *nachash* נחש, whose quality is Trickster. Snake slithers subtly into our lives to stir us toward change, bringing us the blessing and the curse of challenge, of disruption, that then catapults us toward the fork in the road of choice making.

The Hebrew word for Snake, *nachash*, is rooted in the Hebrew word for whisper — חש *chash* — as Snake slithers through our lives quietly, whispering to us rather than shouting at us, so that there is ample room for us to discern, to make solid choices, to choose to listen or to not listen, because Snake is supposed to work in subtleness, not in conspicuousness — otherwise Snake would rob us of our free will. Snake is also about communication, being the first creature in our Creation story to engage another in conversation, thereby inventing dialogue. [28]

NOTES

1. *Midrash Eichah Rabbati* 1:57 and *Eichah Zuta, Nus'cha Bet*, No. 2.
2. *Mishnah, Ta'anit* 4:8.
3. First Chronicles 12:32.
4. Numbers 2:5.
5. *Sefer Yetzirah* 1:1.
6. Genesis 30:14-18.
7. Genesis 35:22.
8. MaHaRaL in *Netzach Yisrael*, Chapter 40, p. 170.
9. Genesis 30:18.
10. Numbers 22:27-28.
11. Numbers 22:31.
12. *Midrash Tanchuma, Balak*, Ch. 9.
13. *Talmud Bav'li, Pesachim* 54a.
14. Zohar, Vol. 3, folio 201b.
15. First Chronicles 12:32.
16. Genesis 22:3-4.
17. Zachariah 9:9.
18. Genesis 22:5.
19. MaHaRaL in *Derech Chayyim*, Ch. 5, folio 267.
20. Genesis 22:3.
21. *Hak'damat Tikunei HaZohar*, folio 12b.
22. *Hak'damat Tikunei HaZohar*, folio 12b.
23. Exodus 24:10.
24. Zohar, Vol. 1, folio 32a and Vol. 3, folio 47b.
25. Deuteronomy 22:10.
26. 12th Century Rabbi Avraham ibn Ezra on Deuteronomy 22:10.
27. *Midrash Bamid'bar Rabbah* 2:9; see also 13th- century Rabbi Yitzchak of Acco in *Sefer M'irat Einayim, Bamidbar*, para. 2.
28. Genesis 3:1-2.

Chapter Seven

Elul

(August 7-October 2)

Elul אלול, meaning: "Full Circle"

Attribute: Health בריאות *b'ree'yoot*

Tribe: Zevulun, זבולון meaning "flow of gift"

Tribal Totem: Seashore יבשה *yabashah* which is about reconciliation of paradox; and creating the space for potentiality of fruition, as in water meeting Earth.

Tribal Stone: Crystal/Diamond יהלם *yahalo'm* whose quality is about bringing respite/sleep

Tribal Herb: Cassia קציעה *keh'tzee'ah*

House: Illness בית החולי *bayt ha'cho'lee*

Zodiac: Virgin בתולה *beh'tu'lah*

Letter: yod י Contained hand

Tribal Flag: לבן White *la'van*, with image of a seafaring boat

Tribal Direction: East, קדם *kedem*, "Beginning," and מזרח *meez'rach*, "Shining"

אלול Elul is the moon that brings us to the moon of transformation, to Tish'ray, the moon of Rosh Hashanah and Yom Kippur, the harvest month, when we experience changes occurring in our natural environment and within ourselves. Elul is the threshold of the passageway to change, the doorway. The harvest season challenges us to either enter the New Year as we are, or to plant fresh seeds in our fields *without* and our souls *within*.

Elul is a challenging month, because it is a bridge, a reaching out, between the full blossoming of Summer and the yet unknown journey of Autumn and Winter. It is about the *end* of a process, as we approach the end of Summer. In fact, Summer in Hebrew, as mentioned earlier, is קיץ *ka'yeetz*, which is also related to the word קץ *kaytz*, which means literally the *end* of something. Because Summer is when all that has grown out of the Earth in Spring, reaches its fullness, its climax, its Ending. But Judaism reminds us that endings are but the seeds of new beginnings. Nature gives us this clue as well, how everything falls from the trees in Autumn, goes into the Earth in Winter, and then miraculously re-emerges anew in Spring! Likewise with Judaism's ancient belief in life after death, or the Afterlife, that when we die here, we are born in another realm, or, at times, reincarnated — sent back here.

> And so does God redeem my soul from crossing into the void, and I can then become aware of my life-ness through the clarity of the Divine Light. Indeed, all these things will God cause to happen with a person, twice, even three times, to bring back their soul from the void toward that light which is in the Light of the Living. [1]

Elul then challenges us to have faith and trust that End only leads to new beginnings. The end of Elul, for example, ushers in the beginning of the New Year, of Rosh Hashanah. So Elul is the month of reaching across the chasm of uncertainty, reaching across the abyss of the unknown, to meet the beauty and gift and blessing of what is waiting to happen next in our lives. In fact, the Hebrew letters that spell Elul אלול actually form an acronym, the initials for four romantic words that appear in King Solomon's sacred Song of Songs — אני לדודי ודודי לי *a'nee l'do'dee v'do'dee lee* — "I am for my beloved, and my beloved is for me."[2] So it is a month of longing, of reaching out to the completely unknown other. Because longing is something we have for the mystery of Other.

In Elul, we prepare ourselves to undertake something new, something different. It is a special month when we dare to reach across what we don't know for sure, in order to receive the gift of what is waiting to come our way. The month of Elul gives us the strength to do this, to reach past our doubts and questions and uncertainties; to reach beyond our worries and anxieties of Future, and instead to welcome Future with the extended arms of a lover.

The attribute of Elul is *be'ree'yoot* בריאות Health. Interestingly, this word is spelled exactly the same as the word for "Creations" — *be'ree'y'ot* בריאות — the blanket term for all the living beings of the universe, whether stone, plant, animal, or human. Health is then about connectivity, the connectivity and harmonious cooperative functioning of the very diverse organs in our bodies as well as the connectivity and harmonious cooperative functioning of the very diverse components that comprise the vast "body" of our universe. Health is about clear communication between the parts that make

up the whole, which is why the first three letters of the word for health, ברי,
spells *ba'ree*, a word that translates as "clear," and the second three letters
spell *o't* אות, one of whose meanings is "signal." Just as clear signals between
the various body parts foster healthy bodies, so do clear signals between
relationship partners foster healthy relationships. Thus, "I am for my beloved, and my beloved is for me."

The tribe associated with Elul is זבולון Zevulun. Zevulun stems from the
word זבד *zeh'vehd*, Hebrew for apportion, as in receiving a nice portion, a
nice gift. His mother was לאה Ley'ah and he was her sixth son. And when he
is born, Ley'ah names him that because she feels that "God has apportioned
me a good portion. Now, perhaps, my man will make a home with me,"[3] still
hoping in the back of her mind that Jacob will one day be as intimately in
love with her as he is with her sister Rachel. Still, hopes and dreams notwithstanding, she maintains as well her independence of Jacob for her happiness.
She says, "God has given *me* a good portion, a good allotment," meaning it is
a gift she claims for *herself*, independent of her connection to Jacob, or of her
hopes for their relationship. Having separated her sense of gift and joy in life
from dependence upon her man through the birth of her last three sons, she
moves more deeply into the power of the feminine, and shortly afterwards
gives birth to דינה Deenah, Jacob's first and only daughter.[4]

The Totem for the tribe of Zevulun is the Seashore יבשה *yabashah* whose
quality is reconciliation of paradox, or seeding, as in adding water to soil.
The seashore is symbolic of boundary, of mutual cooperation, where the land
stops and the waters begin, and conversely where the waters stop and the
land begins. It is about personal space and creating boundaries around that
space that enables the possibility of co-existence between opposites (wet and
dry, land and water, etc.). Both, Water and Earth, when they join in the
delicate dance of union, of intimacy — each continuing to respect where the
other ends or begins and vice-versa — it is only *then* that the two can
conceive together and bring about fruition. If, on the other hand, water over-
runs Earth in an overwhelming way, Earth is blocked from sprouting, from
enabling seed to open and sprout. And, conversely, if there is *not* enough
water, nothing will grow.

Accordingly, Zevulun was assigned the direction of East during the long
desert journey from Egypt to Canaan.[5] East in Hebrew is מזרח *meez'rach*,
which implies "Shining," as East is where the Sun's shining light is experienced anew, and קדם *kedem*, which implies "Beginning." Seashore, the Totem of Zevulun, retains the characteristics of both, ever-renewing and new
beginnings, as the sea continuously shapes and re-shapes the shores, and in
our Creation story it gave birth to land: "And Elo'heem said, 'Let the waters
that are beneath the skies gather to one place, and let the land become
revealed.'"[6]

The stone worn on the breast plate of the ancient High Priest that corresponded to the Tribe of Zevulun is יהלם *ya'ha'lom* — Diamond, or Crystal — which overcomes phobias, spells, schemes by adversaries; also helps with insomnia, and in general brings restfulness to the body. It is usually worn on the left hand or arm.[7] The diamond and crystal represent the blending of the Divine light with the primal elements of Water and Earth, just like the Totem of Zevulun, the Seashore, the meeting of Water and Earth. The solid substance of Diamond represents Earth, and its clear, reflective quality represents Water. Together, these two qualities of Diamond reflect and refract, or translate the light of the Sun, just as Earth and Water translate the Divine Light into the unfolding of Creation. As such, Diamond, like the Totem of Elul — Water blended with Earth — contains within it the conjuring forces of Creation, the power to bring forth potential to fruition.

The herb amongst the sacred incense offering that is related to the tribe of Zevulun and the month of Elul is the Cassia קציעה *keh'tzee'ah* whose medicine is about uprooting, as in preparing a space for fresh seeding, for new growth, in the place of old growth. It's about letting go of what was, to allow for what is and what *can* be. Blended with the other sacred plants of the incense offering it cleansed elements within them that would in any way hinder the fullness of the potential of the plant in terms of its aroma, medicinal potency, and capacity to blend harmoniously and in balance with the other plants. This is actually the traditional ritual practice of the Moon of Elul: it is a period, prior to the beginning of the New Year, when we take stock of the past year and do some introspective work on ourselves to clear out any impediments to our moving on afresh into the New Year Cycle.

The House of Elul is בית החולי *Bayt Ha'Cho'lee*, House of Illness. Remember, this is about the challenge of love, of benevolence we spoke of earlier. Is what we give forth of ourselves draining us? Or nourishing us? This house, then, challenges us to be alert, to be watchful of what and how much of ourselves we pour out to others. Illness is a sign of ebbing, symptomatic of lowering levels of our life force. Illness is also an opportunity to clear out of our bodies what doesn't belong there, to cleanse our systems to allow for renewal of health.

The Shadow House of Elul is בית האיבה *Bayt Ha'Ay'vah*, House of Opposition. The child of Elul, who is often prone to give and do beyond his or her capacity, can meet up with opposition to his or her love and benevolence. And very likely that opposition will come not from without but from within, born out of resentment or frustration; resentment of how much more is expected of them that they can wholesomely give, and frustration over not being able to give or to love as much as they would like! This applies to giving and to loving *oneself* as well as others.

No wonder this moon is smudged with the Cassia, that opens up whole new possibilities This is very much related to the Zodiac for Elul which is

בתולה *Beh 'too 'lah*, or Virgin, the gift of being able to get off the merry-go-round every now and then, and start all over, see everything anew, even the same thing, even the same people, the same situations, the same relationships. It is also about the shedding of old patterns to allow more of the flow of what it is you wish to happen, so that you become not just Water, not just directionless flowing of sea, of ocean, but also the directing power of land, of Earth. So that you become neither exclusively land nor exclusively ocean; neither exclusively with rigid boundaries nor exclusively directionless, but a balance of both, which happens to be the power of your tribal Totem: The Seashore, the blend of flow and containment, flow and containment.

Therefore, the letter of the Hebrew alphabet associated with Elul is the י *"yud"* which is shaped like a seed. Literally, it means "Hand," which, too, contains and allows what is contained to flow forth. Just like the Seed, which contains myriad possibilities of what it then flows forth, of what it then moves toward fruition. In fact, a close look at this tiny letter will yield an image of a flame connecting sky and Earth, spirit and matter, Creator and Creation. Fire itself is fueled from below, drawn from above, symbolic of the yearning for spirit that originates here on the Earth, in our physical realm — again corresponding to the theme of Elul: "I am for my beloved and my beloved is for me." It is a longing we have for what is beyond our reach, for what we know exists beyond our experience, but that we cannot access unless we clear the way, as is written: "Clear the way toward God, smooth-out a pathway to our God[8] ...lift up the obstacle from the path of my people."[9]

Love is sweet as it is painful, all at the same time, something many of us have experienced at some time or another when we were romantically in love, and longed for the presence of a particular person, but they were absent, either physically or emotionally. However romantic and poetic this might be, it also weakens us at times, as our soul — through this deep yearning — sometimes extends herself beyond the boundaries of our physical self. This in turn weakens our bodies and can bring on illness. "I am love sick," declares the un-named lover in Solomon's Song of Songs.[10] Or as the sixteenth-century mystic and poet Rabbi Eliezer Azikri wrote: "My soul has become lovesick from pining for you; please O God, please heal her by revealing to her the sweetness of your radiance."[11]

NOTES

1. Job 33:28-30.
2. Song of Songs 6:3.
3. Genesis 30:20.
4. Genesis 30:21.
5. Numbers 2:7.
6. Genesis 1:9.

7. *Sefer Big'day Kehunah*, p. 38 and on.
8. Isaiah 40:3.
9. Isaiah 57:14.
10. Song of Songs 2:5.
11. *Yedid Nefesh*, Paragraph 2.

Chapter Eight

Tish'ray

(September 5–November 3)

Tish'ray תשרי, meaning: "It shall be smooth"
Attribute: Sexuality תשמיש *tash'meesh*
Tribe: Dahn, דן meaning "discernment"
Tribal Totem: Snake, נחש *nachash*, whose quality is Trickster
Tribal Stone: Jacinth לשם *leshem*, whose quality is self-reflection
Tribal Herb: Spikenard/valerian שבלת נרד *shee'bo'lehd nehr'd*
House: Women בית הנשים *bayt ha'na'sheem*
Zodiac: Scales מאזנים *m'az'nayeem*
Letter: *lamud* ל Teach
Tribal Flag: ספיר Sapphire Blue *sa'pir*, with image of a snake
Tribal Direction: North, צפון *tsa'fon*, "Hidden" "Mystery" "To *Peek* into the Unknown"

Tish'ray תשרי is the month in which Noah first removed the covering of the Ark following the Great Flood.[1] This is recorded to have happened on the very first day of Tish'ray. It is therefore a moon of universal healing and hope, as it was then that Noah dared open the window and remove the veil that had sheltered him and his family and the species of animals they had gathered, and reconnect with the tragedy of a world destroyed. In that reconnection, the healing began and the hope of renewal was restored. In the words of the Zohar:

> It is written: "And Noah opened the window of the ark that he had built" (Genesis 8:7) — this is Yom Kippur; for the Ark of Noah, She is Great

63

Mother, and the window of the Ark is the Central Column, through which the light of the Torah, the hidden light, radiates. [2]

Tish'ray is also a very special month for the Jewish people. It is when we ritually celebrate the harvest season, or as we call it in the Hebrew: *Chag Ha'ah'seef Teh'koo'faht Ha'shanah*—חג האסיף תקופת השנה—"the Festival of the Ingathering at the Turning of the Year."[3] It is Autumn. It is the time when everything goes inward. And we celebrate it in five stages:

1. The first stage, and a very important one, is commitment to newness (Rosh Hashanah ראש השנה)
2. The second stage is letting go of past obstacles (Yom Kippur יום כפור)
3. The third stage is stepping into a place of vulnerability by taking a daring step forward into the uncertainty of future (Sukkot סוכות)
4. The fourth stage is praying for and trusting that good results will come out of this move (Hoshanah Rabbah הושענא רבה). Hoshanah Rabbah is the willow dance ritual that occurs on the last day of *Sukkot*, when we dance around the altar with willows—the willows being representative of our feeling vulnerable around the pending uncertainty of the up-coming Winter. It is a prayer in movement, a prayer for good rains, good outcome of the new seeds we planted in Spring and Summer. And we do this ritual with willow branches, as willows are vulnerable, and need water all the time.
5. The fifth and final stage is שמיני חג העצרת *Sh'meenee Chag Ha'atzeh'reht* (literally: the Eighth Day, the Cycle of Closure), when we lock-in our fortitude, our commitment to trust the process; no more straddling the fences, no more uncertainty. It is a ritual of conviction, of declaring: "Yes! The unknown of the forthcoming Winter moons will reap a good Spring growth in the end."

All of these days, these graduating phases and rituals in the moon of *tish'ray,* are relevant to helping us in our life journey. In the Tenach, they are called by one umbrella name: Rosh Hashanah, literally: "the root or head of trans-formation."[4] This series of festivals, or phases, starts at the very beginning of the month, unlike all the other festivals of the Hebraic tradition. They begin at the first sliver of the moon, and conclude toward the end of the month when the moon begins to wane. They therefore represent whole new begin-nings leading to fullness, and then letting go, trusting the process of waxing and waning in our lives.

Every month on our calendar has a particular quality, a specific attribute. The attribute of תשרי *Tish'ray* is Sexuality, union of body and soul, of body with body—love, intimacy, connection that is played out not only in the heart but also with our physical senses. In the Sephirotic Tree, or Tree of Life, it is the branch we know as *Ye'so'd* יסוד, which literally means Foundation, and also implies "The Secret of Something," from the word סוד, secret - the elusive essence of a thing. *Ye'so'd* relates to sexuality because it is in that arena of human experience and action that our deepest self emerges, is tested, is challenged, and is brought to fruition.

The tribe associated with Tish'ray is Dahn דן, which translates as discernment, or judgment. He is the first of Rachel's sons through her helper-companion Bil'hah בלהה. Rachel רחל was at first unable to conceive, and so with her permission, Bil'hah joined with Jacob and gave birth to a son whom Rachel names Dahn, "For God judged my situation and also heard my voice; and gave me a son."[5] This was not uncommon back then, that a woman unable to bear children would ask another woman to do so on her behalf.

In naming Dahn, Rachel introduced two separate ideas around our relationship with God: (1) that God at times intervenes in our lives in response to *God's* judgment of our circumstance in the moment, and (2) that God at times intervenes in our lives in response to *our* calling out for what we need in the moment. In other words, sometimes God helps us out even if we do not call out, do not pray - simply in response to a judgment of our situation, as it is written: "And it shall come to pass that before they have even called out, I have already answered; before they have spoken, I have already heard."[6] Like the name of his half-sister, Deenah דינה, *Dahn* translates as Discernment, Judgment. Trust your judgment. Dahn is the tribe from which Samson came from. Samson (Sheem'shon—שמשון) lived a very independent lifestyle, very free-flowing, yet he was also involved deeply with the community, as supreme judge and decision-maker for all the tribes. He represents the balance of both lifestyles, independent and free-flowing, *and* commitment and responsibility to the community.[7]

The tribal totem for Dahn, and therefore also for the month of Tish'ray, is Snake, *nachash* נחש, whose quality is Trickster, as we see in the words of First Woman who says, *ha'nachash hee-shee-ah'nee* [הנחש השיאני] "the snake *tricked* me."[8]

There are many challenges that play with us, that come at us when we least expect it. Snake challenges us to take on surprises, to dare—even if it turns out not to be what is right for us—to at least give it a try and surrender a little to the adrenalin we get from new and boldly daring ventures. The snake calls our bluff, tests our convictions, keeps us moving. Snake crawls on its belly, but keeps us on our feet.

After persuading First Woman to eat the forbidden fruit in the Garden of Eden, Snake is told by God: "On your belly you shall crawl and you shall eat dust all the days of your life."[9] This seems at first to be a strange consequence, when we think about it. If Snake has to crawl on his belly with his mouth level with the Earth, then it would seem that he has an infinite and easily accessible supply of what he needs to sustain himself! He doesn't have to climb up, or burrow down, or raise his neck or lower it. His food is right in front of his eyes. But as the 19th-century Rebbe Menachem Mendel of Kotsk explained: "This is the most terrible consequence of all. Because if everything I need is instantly available or easily accessible, then there is nothing for which I *yearn*! And yearning is the bridge between myself and God!"

Snake robbed us of our yearning. He gave us all we wanted in that moment right on a platter. He let First Woman get as far as *admiring* the tree before he convinced her to eat from it, without allowing her to *yearn* for it, which would have come next. She was only given to the experience of (1) the tree seeming okay to eat from, (2) admiring what it looked like, (3) and feeling the intellectual inspiration that it exuded, before plucking its fruit—but she never reached the place of actually yearning for it, desiring it, wanting it, longing for it: "And the woman saw that the tree was good to eat of—and that it was alluring to the eyes, and that the tree itself was inspiring to the mind."[10] So it was intuition, imagination, and inspiration, but lacking the final and most vital ingredient: passion, yearning, longing—*T'shu'kah* תשוקה. And so, in consequence, Snake was deprived of yearning and assigned to become the *catalyst* for all human yearning, to make sure we yearn, we long, we want, and that we don't fall asleep and end up doing things because of succumbing to the pressure of others.

The idea of longing to connect, to unify, is the deeper meaning behind what we refer to as Love, אהבה *ahavah*. It is the soul's yearning to connect with the Greater Soul, or Great Spirit, not because of something that God did for us, or in the hope of what God *might* do for us. The response of Other to our yearning toward them happens when that yearning is not contingent on anything, but is pure and without agendas and expectations. God does not come down to the mountain, so to speak, until Moses goes up. First it is written, "And Moses went up to Elo'heem,"[11] and only then does it say, "And God descended upon the mountain of Sinai."[12] God responds to our *te'shukah*, to our longing, our yearning.

And so, Snake slithers subtly into our lives to stir us toward change, and hopefully to awaken within us passion, yearning, bringing us the blessing and the curse of challenge, of disruption, that then catapults us toward the fork in the road of choice making. The Hebrew word for Snake, נחש *nachash*, is rooted in the Hebrew word for whisper—חש *chash*—as Snake slithers through our lives quietly, whispering to us rather than shouting at us, so that there is ample room for us to choose to listen or not to listen, because Snake is supposed to work in subtleness, not in conspicuousness—otherwise Snake would rob us of our free will. As mentioned previously, Snake is also about communication, being the first creature in our Creation story to engage another in conversation, thereby inventing dialogue.[13]

Snake is a vital catalyst, since without the Trickster in our lives, we tend to atrophy, to become stuck, and our life flow gets sluggish. Snake redeems us from bondage to the hum-drum, bondage to stoicity and numbness. No wonder that the Hebrew word for Snake, *Nachash* נחש , shares the same גמטריא *Gemmatria*, or numerical value, as the Hebrew word for Messiah— *Ma'shee'ach* משיח—358.

Nachash also implies a particular act of sorcery mostly interpreted in the English vernacular as "divination." Its rites involve magical bowls or sticks or rocks or other shamanic implements intended for unlocking the hidden realms of the spirit world.[14] There are various opinions about what consti- tutes the Torah's prohibition around *na'chay'sh* נחש, as it is called, or what kinds are permitted and what kinds are forbidden. The twelfth-century Rabbi Moshe Ibn Maimon [Rambam/Maimonides] prohibited it altogether, while his contemporary, the kabbalist Rabbi Avraham ibn Daud, permitted certain uses of it[15] based on the Talmud's discussion of the issue.[16] Basically, it is, like the word implies, a "tricky" practice, since it could bring deeper *clarity*, or introduce more *confusion*. It is therefore important for one to be grounded and to have done extensive inner work of refining the ego, and to go into this realm with a purity of heart while unattached to a particular outcome. It is also imperative to be associated with a qualified teacher or colleague during the process.

> Not everyone is qualified to approach the mysteries of Torah, which requires battling with whatever wrongness lingers within us. Only then—after one has worked strenuously on one's character—can one achieve the fullness of the wisdom and gift of true wholeness. You should not think that anyone who wishes to leap into the mystery realms can simply do so, and that you can know the wisdom of the unknown without mastering first the wisdom of the known. So many of us simply want to jump into the mystery realm without working on ourselves first, wanting to skip basic wisdom and discipline and immediately study Kabbalah. Of such it is written: "Woe onto the one who builds his house void of balance; and his upper chambers without good judg- ment" (Jeremiah 22:13).
>
> Rather, you must enter this realm of study in its proper sequence: first through the courtyard, then into the house, then to the upper chambers, and then within the chambers of chambers. But if you wish to jump ahead of the cycles and leap straight into the chamber within chambers of the upper realms without cleansing what is unwholesome within you and without removing the impedi- ments that block your inner vision—know that you will taste the flaming swords of the Cherubim who are assigned to guard the path to the Tree of Life (Genesis 3:24). After all, who can taste the nut without first breaking off the shell?[17]

It is no wonder, then, that Dahn was assigned the direction of North during the 40-year desert journey.[18] North in Hebrew is צפון *tsa'fon*, literally: "Hid- den." It is the place of Mystery, the unfinished sentence, the blank space waiting to be filled in by our choices and actions in the moment. The ancients tell how God deliberately left North incomplete, as if to declare: "Anyone who thinks themself as God, let them step forth and finish North."[19]

The stone for the tribe of Dahn is the *Leshem* לשם, or Jacinth. And like the stone Totems of the other Hebrew tribes, this one too was sewn into the breastplate of the ancient High Priest of Israel.[20]

The *Leshem* stone is known to aid in the treatment of insomnia. Tish'ray beckons us to release our burden, whether of guilt of past or anxiety of future, and embrace the sleep and coziness of Winter with faith. To help us do this, we go outside and eat and sleep in our סוכה *sukkah*, our temporary abode during this moon. The *Leshem* stone also promotes spiritual insight and understanding. Since ancient times, it was used as a traveler's amulet, and is believed to help keep you from getting sick when worn on an extended journey.

The herb associated with *Tish'ray* is the *shee'bo'let* שבלת, the valerian, which is the ear of the barley stalk, as in an ear of corn. It is the protective sheath around the barley and represents our need to protect our hearts, our most vulnerable places, especially during *Tish'ray* when, after beating our chests and making commitments to do better, we might find ourselves vulnerable and raw. It also carries the medicinal quality of calming the anxiety one might have in birthing new experiences, or seeding new encounters. This plant is therefore good for placing around newborns, to bring calmness to their newly arrived souls, a kind of welcoming fragrance which brings reassurance that in a way further escorts the newborn through the passageway of transition from the womb world into this world, as well as the soul of the newborn from the spirit world to the physical world. Valerian also has a calming effect and is helpful when suffering from insomnia, just like the stone of this month, the Jacinth.

Even for those of us who have traveled this life time over many decades, it is healing to have moments of rebirth, or being reminded of the welcoming our souls received in coming into this realm, or being gifted with that welcome if we never had received it. In the sacred incense mix, *shee'bo'let* served to resolve any disparity between the spirits of the various plants to help forge the blending. Once again, the concept of intimacy is involved. Intimacy grows out of love, and then anxiety sets in, the fear or concern around whether the intimacy and its loving components will last, will endure. This is why the ingredient of Yearning, Longing is so vital. Soul-deep connection arises out of pure knowing as opposed to contingencies and agendas which are here today and gone tomorrow. "All love that is contingent upon a particular something," the ancients taught, "if that something expires, so does the love. A love that hinges on nothing, however, endures forever."[21] And of course, abuse in the *guise* of "love" is totally unacceptable.

This is the theme of *Tish'ray*. This is why Rosh Hashanah and Yom Kippur happen then, a cycle of time where God reminds us of her love for all creations, a love that is unconditional, a love flowing with forgiveness, understanding, and acceptance. A love born out of yearning, the yearning to create and the yearning that what was created will continue to flourish.

The House for *Tish'ray* is *Bayt' Ha'Nah'sheem* בית הנשים, "*House of Women.*" What brings forth life is Woman, the feminine. This is why the language of the beginning of our Creation story incorporates the feminine force of Creator as the active component that translates Creator's will for Creation to become: "And the Spirit of Elo'heem, She hovered over the waters"[22] —in the Hebrew: *meh'rah'cheh'feht* מרחפת implying that it was the feminine force that initiated the stirring of the seeds of new beginnings into realization. This is the power of Woman. She takes the potential, the seed, and nurtures it to realization. In fact, the Kabbalah clearly implies that Elo'heem אלהים, the only name of God mentioned in our Creation story, "She is *ey'ma ee'la'a* אימא עלאה—Mother of the Above."[23]

There are four realms within this House:

1. The first is the realm of Batyah בתיה, the daughter of the Pharaoh, who adopted Moses as an infant, having pulled him out of the river when he was a babe. She named him Moses—*Moshe* משה—empowering him with the attribute of "drawing forth," which is what the word *Moshe* means.[24] She thereby gifted him with the skill and power of drawing forth our ancestors from out of their bondage in Egypt.

2. The second is the realm of Seh'rach שרח the daughter of Asher, and granddaughter of the Patriarch Jacob, who broke the news to her grandfather about Joseph still being alive. She did this through dance, song, and storytelling. Tradition has it that Jacob still didn't believe the news and jokingly said to Seh'rach, "Sure. Joseph is alive like you are going to live forever."[25] And so she did. And indeed we find her mentioned in the Torah among those who went down into Egypt and among those who centuries later *left* Egypt.[26] It was she, the Talmud tells us, who was therefore able to show Moses where the bones of Joseph were buried.[27] Because our ancestors refused to leave Egypt until the remains of Joseph were found, bound as they were to the promise that *their* ancestors had made to Joseph before he died: that they would take his bones with them back to the Hebrew homeland.[28]

3. The third realm is that of Yo'cheh'vehd יוכבד, the mother of Moses, who hid him from the Egyptians when they were under orders to kill all newborn Jewish males.[29] She then sent him afloat on the river in a basket, and that is when the Pharaoh's daughter took him in. At the advice of Moses' sister, Miriam מרים , the princess hired Yo'cheh'vehd, Moses' mom, to nurse him.[30] According to the oral tradition of the Jews, Moses' mother had originally named him Avig'dor אביגדור,[31] which means "Father of [אבי ah'vee] Boundary, or

Structure [גדור g'dor]" which later empowers Moses with the gift of furnishing the Israelites with *structure* in their lives. She basically is deeply involved in Moses' life, but from behind the scenes.

4. The fourth realm is that of Devorah דבורה, one of the Israelites' highest prophets, who ruled all twelve tribes in unison some 3,200 years ago. Devorah held court not in a building, not even in a tent or hut, but in the shade of an old palm tree.[32] She was also a respected warrior whose vision led the Hebrews to victory over an otherwise unbeatable enemy at the time, led by a Canaanite warlord named Sis'ra, who continuously ravaged and pillaged the fledgling Jewish settlements.[33] Devorah is known for her song, the Song of Deborah, a warrior's song.[34]

These realms of women are in the spirit world. They are described in the Jewish mystical Book of the Zohar as four of the seven heavenly realms, and they are run exclusively by women, particularly by these four women.[35] The difference between the realms, the Zohar tells us, is that in those of Batyah the daughter of Pharaoh and Seh'rach the daughter of Asher, the women there are visited daily by the spirit of the men who benefited from the actions of these two women, and who then gather with them to share mystical wisdom: Moses in the house of Batyah, Joseph in the house of Seh'rach.

Once a day, Batyah welcomes Moses and proclaims to all the women gathered in her realm: "Behold! Here comes the jewel I was honored to polish, the Man of God I was privileged to raise."

Once a day, Seh'rach welcomes Joseph and proclaims to all the women in her realm: "Behold! Here comes Joseph. Happy am I that I was privileged with the honor of informing our grandfather that he was still alive, and later directing Moses to Joseph's bones so that the promise might be fulfilled."

However, in the house of Yo'cheh'vehd, the woman who played a major key role behind the scenes of Moses' birth and upbringing, there are no visitations. What happens there, the Zohar tells us, is song. Yo'cheh'vehd leads the women of her house in song—in particular, the song of her daughter Miriam[36] —and her voice stirs all the souls of men and women in all the other heavenly realms and inspires them to join simultaneously in sacred lovemaking that in turn stirs up lovemaking below as well, on the Earthly plane.

Once again, Yo'cheh'vehd influences life from behind the scenes. She represents the Divine presence in our lives, overseeing, supporting, empowering, from behind the veil, from the *olam ha'nees'tar* עולם הנסתר , the universe of mystery and concealment.

In the realm of Devorah, the prophetess leads the women in her realm in song, the same song she sang when she was alive on Earth.[37]

It follows, therefore, that the Shadow Moon for Tish'ray is the month of Nee'sahn ניסן and the House of Aliveness. Nee'sahn is about liberation, and commemorates the ancient Hebrews' liberation from enslavement in Egypt 3,300 years ago. Slavery notwithstanding, Egypt had been their home for several centuries. At least there they had food and water, and shelter from the Sun—they had stability, even though it was harsh. The alternative of freedom sounded attractive, but at the same time, the process involved in that alternative felt intimidating. Likewise, with the freshness of renewal in Tish'ray comes the anxiety over actually leaving behind parts of us that were comfortable, although not necessarily wholesome, yet familiar and predictable nevertheless. That is how Nee'sahn feels with all of its promises for better tomorrows and liberation from enslaving patterns of yesterday. The promise of liberation introduced so many uncertainties, so much anxiety, leading of course to frustration, anger, and in the process, the shattering of appreciation of the miracles the people witnessed daily through Moses, Aaron and Miriam.

House of Women clashes often with House of Aliveness in that the feminine force in life is what brings *forth* new life, to begin with. And soon after coming into its own, new life often turns against the very womb that brought it to fruition. On a grand cosmic scale we witness this in the discrepancy between Creator and Creation, how Creation takes on a life of its own that is largely in antithesis to our understanding of Creator's intent. Creator made life and beauty and pleasure. Creation often turns it into death, devastation, and suffering. And on a more earthy scale, we see it played-out in the daily drama of the struggle between parents and children.

Meditating on the various realms of the House of Women can be a helpful practice in bringing this struggle into balance.

You might want to visit the house of Batyah to help you draw forth a new way of being that is more fluid and nurturing, like Moses being drawn out of the fluidity of the waters of the very nurturing Nile River.

You would visit the house of Seh'rach to inspire you to celebrate your experiences in song, dance and story. Approach this house to reveal that which is hidden, to uncover more and more of the potentials that lie deeply buried in your dreams, in your hopes, so that you might be free to leave whatever might be holding you back, to leave your personal Egypt if you find yourself stuck there.

You might visit the house of Yo'cheh'vehd to be reminded that your original self lurks behind the scenes always, and if you listen carefully you might hear the song of your soul, whose crescendo will help put your fragmented self back together again whenever you might feel separated from your deepest self.

Finally, you might visit the house of Devorah, to give yourself the courage you need to overcome even the most overwhelming obstacles and challenges in your life, and to sing as you struggle, just as Devorah led the people in song as they struggled against overwhelming adversaries back then.

When you are ready, and you know which house or houses you want to visit, close your eyes, and focus on the lights behind your eyelids. They are your journey vehicles. Study them for a while. Then choose one and breathe yourself into it. Inhale it into you, and you into it. Then journey with your breath, moving yourself deeper and deeper inside of the universe beyond you that lies within you, moving yourself deeper and deeper with each inhale and exhale. Imagine yourself arriving at any one of those houses of Women that you feel would be most helpful in your struggle. When you are done, inhale and exhale your way back into your Self, into where you are sitting or lying, and then back into the lights behind your eyelids. [38]

The corresponding Zodiac quality for Tish'ray is *"ma'az'nayeem"* מאזנים – Scales, which is about choice, weighing our choices. It isn't so important, taught the 18th-century Rabbi Nachmon of Breslav, that we be totally clear about what is right for us in tipping our scales of choice to one side or the other. In other words, it isn't so important which road we take when we stand at the crossroads of choice. What *is* important is (1) that we take a step, onto *any* road, in *any* which direction, and (2) whether it leads us to the right place or not, the challenge is then to find something positive to do once we get there. [39]

The letter for Tish'ray is *Lamud* ל, which implies teaching, education, learning. There is always new learning lurking in the approaching shadows of Winter, in the season of the ingathering, the season of going inward. Since this is a month when we renew ourselves, we are reminded to also open ourselves to fresh learning, fresh perspectives, which would aid us in moving forward in furthering ourselves so that we would be less likely to slip back into the very patterns we prayed and worked so diligently to be released from during the Rosh Hashanah-Yom Kippur process.

NOTES

1. Genesis 8:13.
2. *Tikuney Zohar, Tikun* 39, folio 79b, or 22a.
3. Exodus 34:22.
4. Ezekiel 40:1.
5. Genesis 30:6.
6. Isaiah 65:24.
7. Judges 16:31.
8. Genesis 3:13.
9. Genesis 3:14.
10. Genesis 3:6.
11. Exodus 19:3.
12. Exodus 19:20.
13. Genesis 3:1-2.
14. Genesis 44:5 and 15; Leviticus 19:26.

15. *Mishnah Torah, Hilchot Avodat Ko'chavim* 11:4.
16. *Talmud Bav'li, Sanhedrin* 67b and *Chulin* 95b.
17. 16th-century Rabbi Chayyim Vidal in his introduction to *Etz Chayyim*, toward the end.
18. Numbers 2:25.
19. *Midrash Pirkei D'Rebbe Eliezer*, Ch. 3.
20. Exodus 28:19.
21. *Mishnah Avot* 5:16.
22. Genesis 1:2.
23. *Tikunei Zohar*, folio 88b.
24. Exodus 2:10.
25. *Midrash Alfa Beita D'ben Sira, Keta* 78.
26. Genesis 46:17 and Numbers 26:46.
27. *Talmud Bav'li, Sotah* 13a.
28. Genesis 50:25; Exodus 13:19.
29. Exodus 1:22.
30. Exodus 2:2-10.
31. *Midrash Vayeek'ra Rabbah* 1:3.
32. Judges 4:5.
33. Judges 4:2.
34. Judges Chapter 5.
35. Zohar, Vol. 4, folio 167b.
36. Exodus 15:20-21.
37. Judges 5:1.
38. *Tikunei Zohar*, folio 50a.
39. 18th-century Rabbi Nachmon of Breslav in *See'chot Ha'RaN*, Ch. 85.

Chapter Nine

Chesh'von

(October 5-December 2)

Chesh'von חשון, meaning "reckoning/figuring"

Attribute: Smell ריח *rey'ach*

Tribe: Naf'talee נפתלי meaning "wrestling"

Tribal Totem: Gazelle, אילה *ayalah*, whose quality is agility and spirituality

Tribal Stone: Agate שבו *sh'voe* whose quality is balanced walk

Tribal Herb: Saffron כרכום *kar'kom*

House: Death בית המות *bayt ha'ma'veht*

Zodiac: Scorpion עקרב *ak'rav*

Letter: *nun* נ Fish

Tribal Flag: אדום קלוש Light Red *edo'm ka'loosh*, with image of a gazelle

Tribal Direction: North, צפון *tsa'fon*, "Hidden" "Mystery" "To *glimpse* into the unknown"

חשון Chesh'von (also known as מרחשון *mar'chesh'von*) is the moon of reckoning and figuring, sitting back and taking it all in after a month-long celebration of the harvest rites and the acclamation to the onset of Autumn when everything has turned inward. Chesh'von marks the first rains that fell during the Great Flood of Noah's time, some 4,500 years ago. [1] The ancients called this month *"ya'rey'ach bool"* ירח בול — the Moon of בול *Bool* — and marked it as the month in which the Temple of Solomon was completed. [2] בול *Bool* is also related to the word מבול *Ma'bool*, the Torah's reference to the Great Flood. But actually, the word בול *bool* itself translates as "decay" and "clumps," as in the clumps of decaying vegetation. It is called the Moon of

75

Decay for that reason, since it is by then well enough into the Fall Season that the fallen leaves have decayed into clusters of decomposing foliage.[3]

For a month that has no official religious celebration or fast day, or any other notable commemoration on the Hebrew calendar, it is actually a very full month. On the one hand, it is the month in which the forty days and forty nights of the rains of the Great Flood began, and on the *other* hand it is the month in which the First Temple was completed! Is there perhaps a *connection* between these two events? Of course! You see, while God *did* promise Noah not to flood the world ever again, remnant rains of the Great Flood continued nonetheless annually. Every year since, it rained forty days and forty nights, only it didn't *flood*. And it wasn't until the First Temple was completed, on the 17th day of *Chesh'von*, that these remnant rains of the Great Flood finally ceased completely.[4]

The month of *Chesh'von* is also the same month in which the Earth emerged again from the waters of the Great Flood and the land began to dry up. On the 27th day of this month is when Noah and his family, and all of the creatures they had taken into the Ark, finally *left* the Ark.[5]

The attribute for this moon is Aroma, which tells you to take some time to smell the roses, as they say, or to smell your food, meaning sit back and take in the events of your life, allowing the moment to digest the past and create more wholesome visioning for the future. Interestingly, the word in Hebrew for smell, for scent, is ריח *rey'ach*, related to the word for spirit, or רוח *ru'ach*. We take in the *rey'ach* to nurture our *ru'ach*. The aromas around us not only nurture and inspire us, but they also *inform* us. The spirit of trees and plants, for example, teach us through the aroma we take in from them. "It is impossible for the world to exist," the fourth-century Rabbi Abbayeh taught, "without the aroma of flowers and plants."[6]

The tribe associated with the Moon of Chesh'von is נפתלי Naf'talee, which means "one who struggles," so named by his surrogate mother, רחל Ra'chel, who at the time was unable to bear children, and struggled to compete with her more fertile sister לאה Ley'ah by having her husband יעקב Ya'akov have a child with her maidservant בלהה Bil'hah. Bil'hah then conceives and gives birth on Rachel's behalf first to דן Dahn, and then to Naf'talee.[7] In naming Naf'talee, Rachel declares: "I have struggled a Divinely-intentioned struggle with my sister, and I have prevailed."[8] What does she mean by "*Divine* struggle"? Wasn't it rivalry between two sisters vying for the attention of Jacob?

Well, actually, no. Ironically, the ancient teachers point out, while Jacob was heads over heels in love with Rachel, nowhere do we read about Rachel being in love with Jacob. Her desire was more so for children. "Give me kids!" she yells at Jacob at one point, "and if not, I am as good as dead!"[9] She needs *children* to feel alive. Jacob needs *Rachel* to feel alive, and Ley'ah needs *Jacob* to feel alive. No wonder Rachel has no problem with trading a night with Jacob for a bundle of mandrakes. And no wonder Ley'ah is often pursuing Jacob.[10] And Rachel is jealous of her sister, the story tells us, because Ley'ah is giving birth to one child after another and Rachel can't.[11] And it *is* a Divine struggle, as opposed to a sisterly squabble. Her struggle is with *God*, not Ley'ah. And she prevails because instead of brooding over what she cannot control, she takes decisive action and implements the alternative of having kids through Bil'hah.

From the tribe of Naf'ta'lee comes the prophetess דבורה Deborah, who leads the tribes not from a throne in a palace but from the shade of a date tree.[12] The warriors of her people are battling at the time with an enemy that outnumbers them, but she envisions in her prophecy that her people will be victorious. When she senses their skepticism about her promise of victory, she acts swiftly and saddles her horse to accompany her warriors in battle. She doesn't sit there and chastise them for not believing her prophecy or for not having faith in God. She simply leads them into battle.[13]

The archetype born of Rachel's struggle and resolution is therefore one of agility — like the Totem of Naf'talee, the *ayalah* אילה, the Gazelle — the capacity to be flexible about what we need or want so that if we cannot *get* it the way we *want* it, we seek alternatives. As the Zohar puts it: "If you are having difficulty lighting a fire by rubbing two sticks together where you are standing, try it elsewhere."[14]

The Gazelle, is about agility and spirituality — the ability to move quickly and in balance through obstacles, quietly and without flaw, deliberately, cautiously, bravely. The Land of Israel was often referred to by the ancients as ארץ הצבי *Eretz Ha'tzvee*, or Land of the Antelope,[15] not because there were any significantly large herds of them in Israel but because, again, they were considered spirit animals for the way they moved,[16] barely touching the Earth as they sprinted across the fields. And so it was another way of saying "Holy Land."

Naftali was then assigned the direction of North during the 40-year desert journey,[17] for North — or צפון *tsa'fon* in Hebrew — is about mystery, spirit, literally: "Hidden." He is named after Rachel's hidden struggle with God who is hidden. He is mystery, elusive, not much is known about him, and his is the only tribe from which emerged a female leader of *all* the tribes (Devorah), representative of the feminine, which in itself is symbolic of the hidden, of mystery. For the feminine force was at the same time the mystery behind the *beginning* of Creation and will become in turn the mystery behind the *climax* of Creation in the end of times. The second-century Rabbi Shim'on bar Yo'chai elaborates on this teaching, that at the beginning of time in the process of Genesis, Creator concealed the power of the Feminine — which is Timing of Expression and Fruition — deep within the Great Void. There, like seed within womb, this force waits for the right timing before emerging to coincide with the need for it within the Created Universe.[18] This strange teaching alludes to the mystery of the Feminine, which will not be revealed and fully known until the World to Come that follows the End of Times. It is then, Jeremiah the Prophet wrote, that "God will have created a new phenomenon in the land, for the Feminine will encircle the Masculine,"[19] meaning the true power and mystique of the Feminine will arise and have its time to shine.

The stone of the tribe of Naf'talee that was sewn into the breastplate of the high priest was the שבו *Sh'voe*, the Agate stone, whose medicine helps one to walk in balance even on uneven terrain, to walk in balance even in disconcerting situations. Balance, after all, is necessary for the agile, graceful sprint of the gazelle. It is not only about speed. It is about maintaining good balance of mind and body while running to and fro in life across the gauntlet of extreme situations that reach out to trip us as we whiz by.

The sacred plant associated with the tribe of Naf'talee is the Saffron — כרכום *kar'kom* — in Hebrew, which is about the unification of opposites. In the incense mix, it was the ingredient of the Saffron that enabled a harmonious absorption by the other plants of elements that would otherwise not blend well. *Kar'kom* is thus also believed in our tradition to wield the power of attraction and has to do with drawing near, creating closeness, intimacy. It has the power to call forth what lies dormant within us that has the potential for establishing intimacy. It is therefore a kind of aphrodisiac of sorts, and in the sacred incense blend, it drew forth from the other plants their most intimate secrets which then allowed for a deeper blend, a deeper intimacy, as happens when we reveal to our partners our deepest mystery.

The House for Chesh'von is *bayt ha'ma'veht* בית המות House of Death. Death is about taking that very gazelle-like leap across what is known and what limits us...into the abyss of the unknown and the uncertain. When we do this, something in us dies. And in the course of that daring leap we smash through the intimidating forces of Fear and Self-Limitation and land empowered yet also possibly wounded, like our ancestor Ya'akov who "crossed over" and wrestled through his fears, and though he won, he also limped.[20] Death is about liberation from where one has been in order to allow for fresh birthing into where one is *going*. This is why Solomon did not say "there is a time to *live* and a time to die," but rather "a time to be *born* and a time to die."[21] Life itself is *always*, and has no opposite. Birth can happen only through death. We died in the spirit world and were born into the womb world. Then we died in the womb world and were born into this world. And one day we will die in this world and be born into...well, we'll see.

Death is also ironically about embracing *life*. One's death has little meaning unless one's *life* has meaning. If one is not able to live in a meaningful way, one is less able to die in a meaningful way. Our ancients taught us that those who take life for granted, therefore, and behave irresponsibly and mean-spiritedly toward others, are considered as dead to *begin* with.[22] So, how we are in life tends to be how we will be in death.

Some 2,300 years ago, Alexander the Great asked the Hebrew sages of the Negev: "If one wishes to die, what should one do?" They replied: "One should *live.*"[23] What they meant, was, embrace *life*, because the quality we invest in *living* later translates into the quality we reap in *dying*. Or as the second-century Rabbi Sh'mu'el admonished his colleague Rabbi Yehudah, who was concerned about his struggle with the material world: "Seize and eat! Seize and drink! For the world that we are leaving behind is like a wedding reception!" — in other words, try to enjoy life while you're here.[24]

The House of Death is therefore richly decorated with the trimmings and gifts of *life*. This décor reminds us that the more we celebrate *living*, the better prepared we will be for the transition to *dying*, because the empowerment gained from the celebration of *life* will carry us through the transition of *death*. When the 18th-century Kabbalist, Rabbi Simcha Bunim of Pesyczka was about to depart from our world, his wife stood by his bedside and broke out in tears. He looked up at her, puzzled, and asked: "Why do you cry? Do you not realize that the purpose of my entire life was so that I might know how to die?" [25]

The Shadow Moon for the month of Chesh'von is the Month of Iyyar אייר, whose House is the House of Money, *bayt ha'ma'mon* בית הממון. This implies that with all of your gazelle-like stealth and alternative thinking, and spiritual inclinations — money remains a challenge. And money's relationship with death lies in its tendency to distract you from the in-the-moment gift of living. The Hebrew letter for your Shadow Moon is the ו *wahv*, which means "hook." So, while the letter of the moon of Chesh'von is the other-worldly נ *nun*, or fish, that of its shadow moon is the adversary of the fish, the hook. Hook is also the antithesis to infiniteness, as it represents hooking us into the finite, into what the *wahv* literally means: "And." "And" belongs in the realm of time, space, and matter, connecting one moment to the next in a steady, ongoing stream, each moment separated from the one before and from the one pending. Spirituality or infinity is the opposite of this. There is no consecutive time. All time is circular, singular, bound up within itself, coming from nowhere and going nowhere. There is no "And" beyond the Created Universe. The openings of virtually all of the narratives of the Torah begin with "And," except for the opening of the Torah herself, which begins with the letter ב *bet*, literally: "within." The *wahv* of your Shadow House is then perhaps telling you that in order to break through the barriers keeping you from its cache of money, of prosperity, you need to unfold your נ *nun* so that it opens itself up a little, extending itself toward the quality of ו *wahv*. In other words, move yourself from within yourself to *beyond* yourself. Rather than fearing that the hook will overpower you and drag you kicking and screaming into *its* world, wrap your fish lips tightly around it and drag the hook into *your* world. Morph the נ *nun* of your birth moon into the ו *wahv* of your shadow moon, and the ו *wahv* of your shadow moon into the נ *nun* of your birth moon. Or, in other words: Work at engaging a relationship. Intimacy. Because that is what the process of relationship and intimacy involves moving from with*in* yourself to with*out*, and bringing what is *beyond* you *within*.

The Zodiac for Chesh'von is the Scorpion, or עקרב *ak'rav*. In the Hebrew tradition, scorpion's medicine is about uprooting, severing us from excessive rootedness so that we don't become complacent and so deeply settled-in and embedded that we can no longer move *on*ward, and further our life walk. Scorpion frees us from self-constrictiveness, shakes us out of our complacency. The venom in its sting represents the poison of our own guilt from wrong choices that seeps through us, formatting us, shaping our opinion of our self, our sense of our self, poisoning us with self-effacement and criticism, putting ourselves down for what we did wrong, even though we have worked it through, or allowing censure by others to shape us in that way.

The letter of your moon, as mentioned earlier, is the נ *nun*, which is two י י *yods* mirroring one another, blending within one another, almost beginning and ending simultaneously with nothing in between, no connectivity across the river of time via the worldly journey of "And" — somewhat the Alpha and the Omega locked in intimate embrace. The letter of your shadow moon, on the other hand, the ו *wahv*, is a single י *yod* extending itself, emerging from with*in* itself to with*out*, bringing Creation into manifestation, into the realm of "And." Both, of course, have their spiritual qualities, the differences being that while ו *wahv* represents the relationship of the spiritual with the physical, נ *nun* represents the relationship of the spiritual with it*self*. The two י י *yods* mirroring one another also reminds us that "as above, so below," that everything in the spirit world is mirrored in the corporeal world, and vice-versa.[26]

NOTES

1. Genesis 7:11; *Midrash Tanchuma, No'ach*, No. 11.
2. First Kings 6:38.
3. *Talmud Yerushalmi, Rosh Hashanah* 6a.
4. *Midrash Tanchuma, No'ach*, No. 11.
5. Genesis 8:14-17.
6. Zohar, Vol. 2, folio 20a.
7. Genesis 30:8.
8. Genesis 30:8.
9. Genesis 30:1.
10. Genesis 30:16.
11. Genesis 30:1.
12. Judges 4:4-5.
13. Judges 4:9.
14. Zohar, Vol. 4, folio 166b.

15. Jeremiah 3:19; Daniel 11:16; *Talmud Bav'li, Gittin* 57a.
16. 11th-century Rabbi Shlomo Yitz'chakee [Rashi] on *Talmud Bav'li, Rosh Hashanah* 13a.
17. Numbers 2:29.
18. Zohar, Vol. 3, folio 201b.
19. Jeremiah 31:21.
20. Genesis 32:23-32.
21. Ecclesiastes 3:2.
22. *Midrash Kohelet Rabbah* 9:4.
23. *Talmud Bav'li, Tamid* 32a.
24. *Talmud Bavli, Eruvin* 54a.
25. *Histalkut HaNefesh.*
26. Zohar, Vol. 2, folio 20a; *Midrash Shemot Rabbah* 35:6, *Bamid'bar Rabbah* 12:8, and *Shir HaShirim Rabbah* 50:25; *Midrash Ma'aseh Bereisheet U'Ma'aseh Mer'kava, Keta Dalet.*

Chapter Ten

Kees'lev

(November 3–January 2)

Kees'lev כסלו, meaning "basket/containment"
Attribute: Dream Journeying שינה (Sleep)
Tribe: Gahd גד meaning "fortune"
Tribal Totem: Lioness לביא *lah'vee* whose quality is power in action
Tribal Stone: Amethyst אחלמה *ach'lamah* whose quality is about dream
    and protection
Tribal Herb: Costus קושט *ko'shet*
House: Pathways בית הדרכים *bayt had'ra'cheem*
Zodiac: Rainbow קשת *keshet*
Letter: *samach* ס Prop, as in support
Tribal Flag: אפור *Eh'for*, Grey with image of a fortress
Tribal Direction: South, נגב *negev* "Cleansing," and *da'rom* דרום "Rising"

Kees'lev כסלו by sound translates as "Containment of the Heart" — as in
Kees Lev כיס לב — and by its exact spelling translates as "A Throne onto
Him" — *kees lo'* כס לו (as in Exodus 17:16). It is the moon in which the
mish'kahn, the sanctuary of the holy Ark of the Covenant, was completed
and set up. [1]

    The attribute of Kees'lev כסלו is Dream Journeying. In Hebrew, the word
for sleep is שינה *Shee'nah,* which also means Transformation, Change, since
we shift consciousness when we sleep, and often transformation happens
when we sleep. It is no accident that we say, "Well, let me sleep on it" when
it comes to making hard decisions. And sleep in turn is about Dream Journeying. Dreams, our ancient sages taught, follow how we choose to interpret

them.[2] So it is always a good idea to interpret and follow your dreams in ways that nurture you and those around you.

On the ancient Hebrew moon wheel, the month of Kees'lev corresponds to the Hebrew tribe of Gahd גד. Gahd literally means "good luck" or "good fortune."[3] When Gahd's mother, Ley'ah, stopped bearing children, she followed her sister Rachel's idea and brought Jacob together with her helper/companion Zil'pah, from whom she hoped to have more children. Zil'pah is actually the one who gave birth to Gahd, which Ley'ah declared was her "Good Fortune" — the meaning of Gahd. Good fortune means you don't have to worry so much, no need for urgency or desperation. The archetype of Gahd is then about tranquility, being laid-back, dealing with things one situation at a time, always knowing that it will somehow all work out in the end.

The Totem for the tribe of Gahd is the Lioness — the *lah'vee* לביא — symbol of responsibility, provider, and commitment to family. Lioness also represents "power in action." Sometimes we can possess great skills and not really bring them forth, not really use them. The quality of Lioness is about power translated into action, as the lioness is the member of the pride that actually goes out to obtain food for the pride. She is a clever and very patient hunter with great precision.

Lioness is also about being in one's power, but not flaunting it, employing it only when needed. She empowers us to not be afraid of becoming what we have the potential to become. Lioness also represents the Fierceness of the Feminine, or *Aza De'Nuk'va* in Aramaic עזא דנוקבא. This is the meaning of the feminine side of the Sephirotic Tree where the branch of the Sephirah *Gevurah* גבורה grows. *Gevurah* is about setting limits, directing unbridled wild flow toward Creation, toward something constructive, something meaningful.

Like the other tribes, the tribe of Gahd too was blessed by its ancestral father Jacob, and later by Moses. Jacob's vision about his son Gahd went like this: "Gahd shall be raided by raiders, but he shall in the end raid them at their heels."[4] Moses' vision about Gahd was a little different, also extolling his lioness-like fierceness, and adding: "His gift of vision enabled him to see only what is prime for him, and there he beheld his role as revered chieftain, and how the leaders of the people are drawn to him because of the rightness of his decisions, which he made according to the will of God."[5]

The archetype Gahd is therefore the power within you to refuse intimidation by whatever harm that has occured to you; to know in your heart that you will eventually nip it in the bud, "raid them at their heels," like the ancestor Jacob put it. This means that the negativity in your life will evade you, flee from you, as you gather the courage and wisdom of Gahd that motivates you to know the gift of who you are, to be proud of your prowess and your uniqueness, and with all that, turn around and face that which necessitates your attention.

The capacity to turn your fears around and transform them into bravery can bring you to a quality of wisdom that empowers you with clarity for sound judgment and decision-making. Because clouded judgment comes from confoundment, confusion brought on by our fears, our uncertainties, rendering us vulnerable. When we turn that around and call on the power of the lioness, we cleanse ourselves of all that clouds us. We wade through the confusion toward the open fields of clarity as we learn how to work with that which intimidates us. Remember it is even more essential for you — more so than for those born in other moons — to work through your personal issues so that what you perceive as clarity, what you think you see as negativity, is in fact an objective truth, and that your motives are pure, or else the fierceness of your words or actions will be misdirected and in turn can come back and bite you.

The stone for your tribe is the Amethyst Stone — *Ach'lamah* אחלמה — which was situated in the Third Row of the breastplate worn by the High Priest in ancient times, the *Kohain Ga'dol* כהן גדול. The amethyst was known to offer protection in battle. The amethyst stone was used not only for protection in *physical* combat but also for protection and support in *internal* struggle. You might notice that within the Hebrew for this stone, *Ach'lamah*, the Hebrew word for dream appears: *cha'lo'm* חלום. It is the Dream Stone, the stone whose power inspires Dream, Vision, Imagination, the precursors of our life stories, our life choices and actions and how they might unfold within the realm of infinite possibility.

The corresponding Sacred Herb for Kees'lev is קושט *ko'shet,* or Costus in English, a spiraling ginger. *Ko'shet* literally translates as "correct," as in the teaching of the second-century Rabbi Shimon bar La'keesh: "Before you *ko'shet* someone — meaning, before you *correct* them — first correct *yourself.*"[6] It is also used to imply "truth" or "straightforward" as this is the herb that guides the smoke of the sacred incense offering to best translate the core truth of intent behind the offering.

Juxtaposed, the word *ko'shet* becomes *sheh'ket* שקט or "silence," the kind of silence that is louder than words, more intimidating than sound. The silence we call "deafening silence," the kind we are suddenly left with following the abrupt ending of loud noise; the calm before the storm kind of silence. In the sacred incense blend, this plant quieted any sizzling that may have otherwise been caused by the smoking plants, by the fire in the stones on which the herbs were mixed.

This is the herb that contributed to the quiet of the incense, eliminating all crackling noises, all noises that did not belong there, making the sacred incense offering an offering of spirit, of silence, of breath without verbiage. It is about knowing when to be silent, when to remain still, when not to react, not to respond, by which power — like the stealth, silent, stalking of the lioness on the hunt — there is resolve. As the ancient rabbis taught: "The world exists solely in the merit of the one who knows when to be silent in a moment of conflict."[7] Sometimes when we speak in a situation when we ought to be silent, in a situation of conflict, we spill our basket, we lose our soul gift, we fuel the fires of animosity and negativity, and the truth of the circumstance could become blurred. Silence is at times intimidating to us in such situations and at times empowering to us: Intimidating when we are silent out of fear, and empowering when we are silent out of wisdom and courage. Like the ancient teachers taught us: "Just as important as it is to speak that which will be heard, it is just as important to not speak that which will *not* be heard."[8]

In the silence is where the truth emerges. "Truth," wrote King David, "emerges from out of the Earth[9] " — Earth being of those Creations known to us as the Still Ones, or *do'mem* דומם.

It's no wonder, then, that the tribe of Gahd corresponds to the Moon of Kees'lev, which translates as Containment of Heart, as in a Basket that holds what is welcome, what is Gift. The attribute of Gahd, of the lioness, is containment of life flow, containment of all that nourishes, while knowing how to block out that which is not helpful in our lives.

The *kees* in *kees'lev* — the basket — in the ancient sense of what is a basket — is open to receive and contain what we wish to acquire, and also has a lid to keep out all that is not desirable and that is threatening to our life gift. We cannot have such a basket quality in our lives without the quality of Gahd, the quality of being willing and able to turn ourselves around from the place of being driven by others to a place of valuing who we are. The Dream Journey person takes chances, accepts the dare, often having to destroy obstacles that block the path, and to do so requires the faith that no matter what comes against you, or what seeks to sabotage your journey, it cannot touch your soul, because your soul, your heart, your holy of holies, is safely contained: *Kees'lev*. Yes, your Holy of Holies is your heart.[10]

At times, then, we must shut the lid on who we are and keep out negative flow. This containment helps us to maintain clear judgment and develop patterns of leadership that are not about ego but about cradling, containing, nurturing others. Our judgment can then emerge not from confusion but from clarity and peace of mind.

The House for Kees'lev is בית הדרכים *Bayt Ha'd'rah'cheem, House of Pathways*, of many opportunities to choose from in your life walk. The House of Pathways therefore sits in the Moon of the Basket, the Moon of Gahd, because only with this empowerment can one look beyond one's subjective self to also see alternatives, options, other ways of looking at the same issue — crucial for anyone in leadership position or the position of counselor or judge. In the clouded place, we can only see an issue in a single color, a single shape. From the place of clarity we can see the many colors of the rainbow of any theme or issue. We can become more attuned to how the one light of the Sun is translatable into many shades and colors, and therefore also how the manifestation of the one God is translatable, too, into endless possibilities, and so with every issue that comes before us for assessment.

With the House of Pathways, we walk our lives with as many possibilities of choice and perspective as there are hours in the day, because we have dropped our fears by the courage of the lioness. And we are therefore emancipated from constrictive ways of seeing things and freed up to see the many in the one, and the one in the many. We are freed by the tension of being held back so that we sling like a bow, like a קֶשֶׁת *keh'sheht*, into the dynamics of life versus the bondage of an otherwise static life.

None of this is possible without the Dream Journey blessing of Kees'lev. It is only by way of our Dream Journey that we can even imagine, even fantasize the possibilities we haven't tackled yet. When we are driven by others, as Jacob put it: "raided by raiders," then we are blocked not only in our life journey but also in our Dream Journey. We become hopeless and our dreams, our hopes are dashed, are discouraged. When, however, we dare to dream the opposite of what we tend to feel, we thereby turn that negative force around and we end up "raiding the raiders at their heels." Without the dream there is no hope. With the dream, we empower ourselves with becoming what we think we cannot become, accomplish what we have feared we cannot accomplish.

Your Shadow Moon is See'vahn, the Gemini Moon, or in Hebrew, *Te'oo'meem* תאומים — the Moon of Twins. Your Shadow Tribe is then that of Ley'vee לוי, the tribe from where our ritual facilitators came, such as the *Ko'hanim*, the priests, and the Levites. This tribe is about zealousness, and extremes, which is why they were assigned as ritual facilitators, so that their zeal could be subdued and in check. They were never assigned their own land when our ancestors settled in Canaan, but were spread across the lands of the other tribes, serving as ceremonial facilitators for each tribe.

Shadow Moon, again, means that the quality inherent in your life walk as gifted by your birth month is prone to be challenged by the quality inherent in the Shadow Month. The tendency and audacity of the Kees'lev child to dream what most would not dream of dreaming, and journey where others might not journey, could sometimes get out of hand and shift to extremes by virtue of the shadow moon of See'vahn. The fierceness of the lioness in the Kees'lev child could spill over into a zeal of fierceness that might be more about viciousness than fierceness. Therefore, the Kees'lev child needs to reinforce her גבורה Gevurah quality to truly contain (כס *kees*) her heart (לב *lev*), to truly be centered while journeying; seated on a throne of sovereignty (כס *kais*) over See'vahn's impulsivity.

Your Shadow Moon, by the way, is the month during which the Torah was given at Sinai. Thus, it is about spiritual or religious zeal, which is good, and which can also be negative when allowed to run its course toward the extreme. This is why the Torah was given in the Moon of Twins, as there are many faces to the Torah, and as a manifestation of Divine Flow it can be used both as medicine for the soul, or poison for the soul.[11]

As Shadow Moons of each other, both Kees'lev and See'vahn also complement one another, and actually *need* one another. Light needs shadow to offset its brilliance, and shadow needs light to give it purpose and shape. So, while the Divine Torah was given in See'vahn, its actualization, its physical manifestation on the Earthly plane did not happen until Kees'lev, because it was in the month of Kees'lev that the *Mishkan*, משכן — the Ark of the Covenant and all of its implements — were completed and set up.[12] The Mishkan, after all, was the physical expression of the spiritual Torah. The Kees'lev child then is gifted with the prowess of the lioness to direct what flows so that the flow does not overflow and begin to flood.

In the ancient Hebrew moon wheel, the Zodiac sign for this month is the Rainbow — *Keshet* קשת in Hebrew, which, again, also translates as Bow. Rainbow teaches us that each of us is a single solitary soul, unique in the universe like the Sun in the sky. Yet, our potentials are many, like the one light of the Sun translating into many colors through the prism of water. Water is that mysterious force in the world that opens up the seed within the Earth and calls forth its possibilities. Water is also symbolic of the unbridled flow of Creation, again which the Kees'lev child has the capacity to direct, to channel, to contain. Just like the word Kees'lev implies Containment of Heart, and Heart, as we know, the seat of our emotions, tends to overflow at times and blur our vision. The *keshet*, or rainbow quality of Kees'lev, then directs the un-directed glow of the Sun light and translates it into seven colors within the waters, within the rain drops or the flowing river or crashing waterfalls.

The colors of the rainbow are:

Red, which is Earthiness, and about passion;
Orange, which combines the passion of *red* with the new beginnings, or creativity, of *yellow*;
Yellow, new beginnings, as in the color of the Sun, and about creativity;
Green, which is a combination of *yellow* and *blue*, new beginnings from Sun — *yellow* — and inspiration from sky — *blue*;
Blue, the color of sky and its reflection in the ocean, the kiss of the upper waters and the lower waters;
Indigo , an *amplified blue* like the Sapphire, which is about deepening one's spiritual awareness;
Violet, which is a combination of *red* and *blue*, sky and Earth, the dance of physicality and spirituality.

The tribal colors for Gahd are Yellow and Emerald Green, and this particular tribe was positioned in the South during the Exodus journey through the desert.[13] South in our tradition is about cleansing, cleaning away all the grime and fogginess that sometimes blocks us from seeing truth. That is where the word *Neh'ggev* נגב comes from: *leh'nah'gev,* לנגב meaning "to cleanse, to wipe clean."

These two colors, yellow and green, are symbolic of Sun and Earth. The Sun — which we see as yellow — brings forth the green of Earth, the vegetation, the life expression of Earth. Yellow and green represent the dance of that which lies dormant within us, and that which calls forth the dream to fruition.

Each moon has a particular Hebrew letter assigned to it. The letter assigned to the moon of Kees'lev is the ס *Sah'mach*, which literally means "Support" or "Prop," something to lean on for support. Walking along the many pathways, the Kees'lev child requires support, something or someone to lean on, to encourage, guide, empower. It is therefore not surprising that the word סמך *sah'mach* also is used to imply connection and association. This is not only about being predisposed by your birth time for receiving and giving support, it is also about faith, about allowing yourself to trust, to lean in, to fall or step into the unknown, into the uncertain, with the faith that you will be supported; to feel deserving of support, and also to feel empowered to be a source of support to others where and when needed.

To be a child of Gahd requires a lot of support. It is not an easy task to turn one's fears into empowerment, to turn one's confoundment into wisdom, to turn one's cloudiness into clarity. The letter *sah'mach* is shaped like a containment ס, a basket, for carrying the quality of Gahd one needs to protect the courage, the clarity, the wisdom, calling on the support of others while having strong faith in God and one's self, thereby creating an ever-expanding circle of support. The *sah'mach* is also shaped like a circle ס. A circle is a very powerful symbol, as it has no sides, no right side or left side, no top or bottom, and no first or last.

The Gahdite needs to maintain constant vigil over her or his convictions, keeping a sacred circle around them at all times, an invisible circle of protection to support what one has attained (like the basket lid) and constantly strengthen that encirclement with rituals and prayers that are not about ego but about truth. Each time the Gahdite reaches a pinnacle of self-realization, of self-empowerment, courage, and clarity, the Gahdite connects that achievement to the Infinite One and recites this mantra:

> Do not be afraid of sudden terror;
> Or from sinister forces when they might come at you;[14]
> They may scheme against you but their schemes will evaporate;
> They may cast their spell against you but they shall not come to pass;
> Because God is with us.[15]

NOTES

1. *Midrash Bamid'bar Rabbah* 13:2.
2. *Midrash Eichah Rabbah* 1:18.
3. Genesis 30:12.
4. Genesis 49:19.
5. Deuteronomy 33:20-21.
6. *Talmud Bav'li, Sanhedrin* 18a.
7. *Talmud Bav'li, Chulin* 89a.
8. *Talmud Bav'li, Yevamot* 65b.
9. Psalms 85:12.
10. Zohar, Vol. 3, folio 161a.
11. *Talmud Bav'li, Yoma* 72b.
12. *Midrash Bamid'bar Rabbah* 13:2.
13. Numbers 2:14.
14. Proverbs 3:25.
15. Isaiah 8:10.

Chapter Eleven

Tey'vet

(December 2–January 29)

Tey'vet טבת, meaning: "in good condition"
Attribute: Agitation רוגז *ro'gehz*
Tribe: Asher, אשר meaning "happiness"
Tribal Totem: Olive Tree, אילן זית *ee'lahn zah'yeet*, whose quality is protection and bounty
Tribal Stone: Beryl תרשיש *tar'sheesh* whose quality is digestion/consumption
Tribal Herb: Aromatic Bark קילופה *kee'loo'fah*
House: Sovereignty בית המלכות *bayt ha'mal'chut*
Zodiac: Kid Goat גדי *g'dee*
Letter: *ayyeen*. ע Eye
Tribal Flag: ירוק כזית *ya'ro'k ke'za'yeet,* Olive Green, with image of an olive tree
Tribal Direction: North, צפון *tsa'fon*, "Hidden" "Mystery" "To *peek* into the unknown"

Tey'vet טבת is the month during which the Babylonian king, Nebu'chad'neh'zar first converged on Jerusalem to destroy her and her Temple.[1] It is also the month during which Esther was accepted as Queen of the Persian Empire,[2] which ultimately led to the *restoration* of the Jewish Commonwealth and the *rebuilding* of Jerusalem and the Temple. So Tey'vet is about upheaval and restoration, destruction and renewal.

The word Tey'vet itself is related to the word for "Good" in Hebrew: *tov* טוב. "Good" in the ancient Hebraic mindset implies that things are as they

ought to be. The term is first used — repeatedly so — in the Hebrew Creation story. After each phase of Creation, the narrative tells us that "God saw
that it was Good" — meaning, as it ought to be.[3] Even the Babylonians
advance on Jerusalem was — unfortunately — "as it ought to be," prophe-
sied years before by the prophet Ezekiel in the same month, the Tenth
Month.[4] Esther becoming queen of Persia may not have been her preference,
but it was as it ought to be, meaning that in the end, it would all turn in her
favor and for the benefit of her people.[5] This theme would ultimately become
a popular mantra amongst the Jewish people throughout their struggles, individually and collectively: "*Gahm zo' l'tovah* גם זו לטובה — This, too, is for
the good," an adage coined by a second-century master we know only as
Nachum. In time, Nachum became more popularly known as Nachum Ish
Gahm Zo' — "Nachum the Man of 'This, too…'"[6] — as in "This, too, is for
the good."

This month teaches us that no matter how bleak and hopeless our circumstances seem to us in the moment, there is a rightness about it hidden deep
within those very circumstances that in due time will emerge and reveal itself
and turn things around for the good. We learn that at some point, what was
destroyed will one day be rebuilt, what has fallen will again rise up. This is
the theme of our people's vision throughout our history, and it is inspired by
the lesson of the Tenth Month, the month of Tey'vet.

The attribute for the Moon of Tey'vet is *ro'gehz* רוגז or agitation. It is a
word that is also used to imply anger. Anger in Hebrew is usually *kah'ahs*
כעס, and *ro'gehz* is sort of the stirring up of emotions that lead *toward* anger,
but may not necessarily *manifest* as anger. Tey'vet is filled with mixed
emotions, the anxiety of things going downhill, mixed with the anticipation
of the promise that "all is as it should be," that in the end things will turn
around for the better. Living in between those two poles makes us agitated,
sometimes angry, impatient, and — paradoxically — hopeful, even happy.

And sure enough, the month of Tey'vet is associated with the Hebrew
tribe of Asher אשר, which literally means "happy," so named by the matriarch Ley'ah who was overjoyed at his birth. He wasn't her biological child
but her surrogate child, born of the womb of her hand-maiden Zilpah.[7] In the
story of Asher's birth, we come to understand the obscure nature of this
happiness. It was a mixed happiness, mixed with a little sadness, or frustration. Ley'ah had been the lesser-loved wife of Jacob, and had struggled to
win more of Jacob's attention by giving him children, something her sister
Rachel — whom Jacob loved more — could not do for a long time. And
when Ley'ah herself ceased to be able to have children, she did some match-
making between Jacob and her hand-maiden Zilpah, so that she could have
more children to her credit, albeit by proxy. So, of course, there were mixed
emotions, happiness and frustration, at the birth of Asher by her hand-maiden
Zilpah. Happy that this additional child was to her credit, frustrated that she

could not have given birth to him herself, which she felt could have increased her favor in the eyes of her husband even *more.*

So Asher is about happiness and Tey'vet is about things being okay, yet both share the common quality of mixed feelings of happiness and acceptance. We see this exemplified later in the story of Asher's daughter Seh'rach, who is assigned the task of breaking the good news to her grieving grandfather Jacob that Joseph is still alive. She has to dance, story-tell, and sing to him in order that the shocking good news would not endanger Jacob's life. She has to dance on a very thin, delicate wire in the name of happiness, and for the cause of setting things right. The ancient rabbis include her as among the few people who went up into the heavens alive.[8]

The Totem for the tribe of Asher is the Olive Tree, which offers shelter from the desert heat, protection from the burning desert Sun, and oil for sacred rites of anointing as well as for wholesome nourishment. In the life of our desert-dwelling ancestors, these and other similar oasis trees were God-sent, and often treated with Divine respect, such as the *asherah* אשרה, the Goddess Tree that stood in the First Temple for close to 300 years. It was eventually ejected from the Temple because people began to worship it too much as a deity separate from the One God. The same fate befell the Copper Snake that Moses made,[9] which also stood in the First Temple until King Chiz'kee'yahu took it away, for the same reason.[10]

The Tree of Asher is about the challenge we undergo when we are gifted with relief from challenge. Do we turn to the shelter and nourishment itself, or to their *source*, to the One who gifted them to us in those moments? Do we thank only the magnificent tree for its shade and its nurturance, or do we also thank the Creator who *made* the tree and guided us to it as we struggled through the merciless desert?

Asher's Tree Totem also represents the conversation of Nature. As the Talmud puts it: "The trees communicate one to the other, and to all creatures."[11] The tree teaches us self-sufficiency, dropping leaves and pine needles to the Earth which eventually creates compost that both absorbs moisture and fertilizes the soil around it that continues to feed its growth. Tree also teaches us that to ascend toward the heavens we need to first root ourselves deep within the Earth, and the more we root ourselves in Earth, the higher toward the heavens we grow.

The stone associated with the tribe of Asher that was sewn into the breastplate of the High Priest in ancient times,[12] is the Beryl, or *tar'sheesh* תרשיש in Hebrew, whose medicinal quality has to do with digestion/consumption, improving your capacity to take in what comes to you, and to do so in a way that is wholesome and nourishing to your body, mind, and spirit. It is also a precious stone that the prophet Ezekiel uses in his attempt to describe his vision of the four heavenly spirit beings, the *O'fah'neem*, אופנים or whirling ones, the ones with the faces of Lion, Eagle, Buffalo, and Human, *ar'yeh,*

neh'shehr, sho'r and ah'dahm אריה נשר שור אדם. He describes their movement and their countenance as "likened onto the glow of the *tar'sheesh*, the
Beryl stone."[13] So this stone is associated with the high beings of the upper
realms who stir Creation into ever-evolving renewal and perpetuation. It is
the Stone of the Merkavah מרכבה, the vehicle or force that moves Creation
through its cycles of chaos, emptiness, darkness, and light — *to'hoo, vo'hoo,
cho'sheh'ch*, and *ohr* תהו בהו חשך אור [14] — the four cycles of Genesis, danced
into existence in every moment by Eagle, Lion, Human, and Buffalo.

Asher was positioned in the North during the 40-year desert trek,[15] imbued with the Wind of *Tza'fon* צפון, meaning "Hidden" and "Mystery." The
oil from his Totem, the Olive Tree, was the sacred implement for anointing,
for initiating, which stems from the place of Mystery, creating in the moment
what is to become from what never was. And, of course, there is the deep
mystery nature of the Beryl stone and its spiritual associations we just
learned about above.

The particular herb associated with the month of Tey'vet, from among the
sacred plants used in the Incense Offering of the *keh'to'reht* קטורת is the
kee'loo'fah קילופה or Aromatic Bark,[16] an important ingredient that marinat-
ed the blend with sweet aroma, an aroma that draws out the spirit of plants or
stones or animals to the surface. This bark calls forth the aromas, the fra-
grances, which is actually the life breath or spirit of the plant or stone,
thereby optimizing the fragrance and the sweetness of aroma in the sacred
incense blend. If one were to communicate with a rock spirit, for example,
one would rub this bark on the stone to create a friendly, inviting venue for
the rock spirit to come forth. The word itself implies "peeling," as in peeling
away what stifles potential sweetness in our lives, just as in the incense blend
the *kee'loo'fah* peels away the layers of the other herbs that veils their deepest gift, their deepest, most hidden sweetness and potency.

The House for Tey'vet is House of Sovereignty, *bayt ha'mal'chut* בית
המלכות. Mal'chut is a complicated word. Mostly we tend to simplify it and
translate it as kingdom or sovereignty. But it is a fully-packed word that
implies Keeper or Guardian of many realms. Just as the Earth is associated in
the Kabbalah with the *sefirah* of מלכות *mal'chut*,[17] because she is the keeper,
the guardian, of many varieties of species of stones, plants, animals, people,
and each their particular needs, environmental and otherwise. She arbitrates,
maintains harmonious balance of all the diverse dwellers who sojourn upon
her and within her. We call this "eco-system."

So the realm or House of *Mal'chut* is a place of incredible responsibility,
a role involving arbitration, harmonization, coordination, peace-keeping, etc.
Something we see personified in the story of Moses and how he tends to the
ever-changing needs of the people, of twelve very different tribes with very
different mindsets and needs, not to mention the many other peoples who
came out with us from Egypt[18] with *their* unique cultural needs and expecta-

tions. Moses is described in the Torah as being busy day and night arbitrating and coordinating, judging and resolving[19] — he is the personification of the House of Sovereignty, *Bayt Ha'mal'chut.*

The prophetess Devorah is another example, described by the Tenach as "Mother to all of Israel,"[20] judge and leader of the entire nation![21] Of course, *mal'chut* brings great honor and praise to those capable of living up to its implications and responsibilities, but it also brings agitation and anger, toward and from the person blessed or cursed enough to carry its responsibilities. No wonder that Moses argued with God for hours, trying to get out of the assignment of *mal'chut* thrown at him at the Burning Bush. "Please!" he pleaded. "Send someone else! *Anyone* but *me!*"[22]

The key to doing this work, to live in the House of *Mal'chut* without going stir crazy, is to go stir crazy. While the power of *mal'chut,* of rulership, drove Israel's first king, Sha'ul, insane, it was precisely insanity that made his successor David a more successful heir to the throne. Rather than allowing power to drive him insane, as happened to Sha'ul, David uses insanity to stabilize his power. He behaves out of the norm on three occasions: (1) when he dares to challenge the well-armed giant warrior Gol'yat (Goliath), armed only with a home-carved slingshot and a single stone[23] (2) when he behaves like a madman in order to disguise his identity and escape his Philistine pursuers;[24] and (3) when he dances and whirls wildly and half-naked down the main streets of Jerusalem in celebration of the return of the Ark of the Covenant after it had been captured by the Philistines.[25]

"Give me a little craziness," David asks God. "I know you created it, too." And from letting himself go wild and crazy, David sees that it can bring one to a state of ecstasy, a place of joyfulness. "Wow!" David declares to God afterwards. "What a great thing is this craziness that you created." He then wrote Psalm 32, which opens up with "I will acknowledge God as the Source of Blessing for all moments" — to which the *Midrash* adds: "For moments when *wisdom* is appropriate and for moments when *craziness* is appropriate."[26] Behaving outside of the norm, outside of the box, can at the right times be helpful and sometimes even necessary.

A little craziness, a little dose of letting go of protocol and getting wild, goes a long way in keeping your *mal'chut* in a good place and bringing balance to the sometimes overwhelming drive of being in charge, and its accompanying agitation.

The Shadow Moon for Tey'vet is Tamuz and the House of Ancestors. While the child of Tey'vet seeks to reign, influenced by the House of Sovereignty, the Shadow House of Ancestors will at times shatter the illusion of sovereignty by reminding the Tey'vet child that they are not the Alpha of all that they have achieved, but are rather the "tip of the iceberg." Those born in Tey'vet are then challenged to take stock of their capabilities, not be overridden by their failures, but to focus on and build upon their achievements, their talents, their unique selves. All of our ancestors, the Torah shows us, had their moments of failure, of falling, but never did they allow those failings to stop them dead in their tracks. They moved on, they moved through it all, and thereby became ancestors, models, exemplifying to us how to walk through blizzards, traverse storms, and rise up like the Phoenix from out of the ashes, again and again. The Shadow House of Ancestors can be intimidating to the Tey'vet child of the House of Sovereignty, but it must be remembered that the House of Ancestors can actually be just as empowering as it can be humbling.

No wonder that the Zodiac attribute for Tey'vet is the *g'dee*, גדי the kid goat, the quality of playfulness, a quality that — like the kid goat — brings one agility, flexibility, and fine-tuned balance in the otherwise serious and busy environment of the House of Sovereignty. The kid goat reminds us to dance, to skip and jump gleefully over the hurdles and obstacles that tend to clutter the House of Sovereignty with all of its challenges and responsibilities, with all of its have-to's. The kid goat reminds the Tey'vet child to take time to play, to celebrate life, not only take care of obligations. Take time to skip, to dance, to play. To run wild. To throw all caution to the wind like David did after recapturing the Ark of the Covenant.

The letter associated with Tey'vet is the *ah'yeen* ע which means Eye. It also means Wellspring (עין *ayn*), as the eye is the wellspring from which our knowing trickles forth, our perspective, our awareness. It is the core point of choice-making, subject to change at any moment's notice based on what we perceive, what we experience, how we in any given moment choose to interpret what we see or feel, or how we choose to allow what we see to influence us, emotionally, physically, spiritually. In the Kabbalah, the eyes are considered the window of the soul, and that one can see into the soul of another by gazing deeply into their eyes. They are also sometimes referred to as the "Communal Elders."[27]

As the lenses of the soul, our eyes not only receive what is in front of our line of vision but also enlighten us with fresh perspective, as happens with Adam and Eve in the Garden after they eat of the forbidden fruit. There it is written: "And the eyes of them both opened,"[28] or in the story of Hagar, who is feeling hopeless and about to give up when God "opened her eyes and she saw a wellspring of water"[29] after she had run out of water during her desert journey with her son Yish'ma'el. We also find it written about Abraham, Isaac, Jacob, Joseph, Joshua, David — and even Bil'ahm the Midianite prophet who was hired by the Moabites to curse the Israelites: "And he lifted up his eyes and he saw."[30] The implication is, that they experienced some sort of epiphany that shifted their perspective and brought them fresh clarity; they saw things differently, lifting their perspective of things above the way in which they had been accustomed to seeing. In the words of the Zohar:

The eyes weave us through the universe of dream and the universe of reality. When we shut our eyes, we dream, when we open them we realize. When we shut our eyes, we veil the obvious in order to see into the mystery, and when we open our eyes we veil the mystery in order to see into the obvious. The letter ע itself has two wings, two extensions, representative of the two ways in which the eye sees, when it is shut and when it is open. [31]

In other words, they bring to us what we are accustomed to knowing, and they reveal to us what we have not known before. And with ample spiritual work, one can see *both* ways, with our eyes either open or shut.

NOTES

1. Second Kings 25:1.
2. Esther 2:16.
3. Genesis 1:4,10,12,18,21,25.
4. Ezekiel 4:1-2.
5. Esther 4:14.
6. *Talmud Bav'li, Ta'anit* 21a.
7. Genesis 30:13.
8. *Talmud Bav'li, Kalah Rabatee*, Chapter 3.
9. Numbers 21:9.
10. Second Kings 18:4.
11. *Midrash B'reisheet Rabbah* 13:2.
12. Exodus 28:20.
13. Ezekiel 1:16.
14. Genesis 1:2.
15. Numbers 2:27.
16. *Talmud Bav'li, K'ree'tut* 6a.
17. *Tikunay Zohar*, folio 104b.
18. Exodus 12:38.
19. Exodus 18:13.
20. Judges 5:7.
21. Judges 4:4-5 and 5:7.
22. Exodus 4:13.
23. First Samuel 17:49.
24. First Samuel 21:14-16.
25. Second Samuel 6:16.
26. *Midrash Tehilim*, 34:1.
27. Maharal in *Chidushei Agadot*, Vol. 3, *Mesechet Sanhedrin*, folio 138.
28. Genesis 3:7.
29. Genesis 21:19.
30. Genesis 18:2, 22:4, 24:63, 33:1, 43:2; Numbers 24:2, Joshua 5:13, First Chronicles 21:16.
31. Zohar, Vol. 3, folio 280b.

Chapter Twelve

Sh'vaht

(January 1–February 28)

Sh'vaht שבט, meaning scepter and tribe

Attribute: Taste ליטה *l'ee'tah*

Tribe: Joseph, יוסף *yo'sef* meaning "Shall Increase"

Tribal Totem: Wild Donkey פורת *po'raht* and Buffalo שור *shor* — independent and unwavering

Tribal Stone: Onyx שהם *sho'hahm* with the quality of charisma/illusion/delusion

Tribal Herb: Smoke-Raising Herb מעלה עשן *ma'aleh a'shahn*

House: Love בית האהבה *bayt ha'ahavah*

Zodiac: Pitcher דלי *d'lee*

Letter: *tzadee* צ Balanced/Righteous

Tribal Flag for Efrayim son of Joseph: שחור עד מאוד Very Black *sha'chor ahd me'o'd*, with image of a Buffalo, *shor* שור, whose quality is family ties, relationships.

Tribal Flag for Menasheh son of Joseph: שחור עד מאוד Very Black *sha'chor ahd me'o'd*, with image of an Oryx, *reh'aym* ראם, whose quality is power and agility.

Tribal Direction: West, מערב *ma'arav*, "Blending"

שבט Sh'vaht is related to the Hebrew word for Tribe, *shay'vet*, שבט, and it also means Scepter, as in the staff that the tribal leaders would carry as a symbol of their leadership, their role as being the primary source of support and counsel for the people in their tribe. This moon appears during the crescendo of Winter, the peak phase of the Earth's pregnancy when her seeds begin to move toward the passageway of emergence, similar to the unborn child starting to kick inside the womb. It is believed to be the beginning of the first flow of the sap in the trees, of the tree's life force awakening potential fruition out of the deep sleep of Winter. The ancient masters were in dispute only insofar as when exactly this process began, but it was unanimously agreed that it was during the Moon of Sh'vaht, which became known as ראש השנה לאילן *Rosh Hashanah La'Eylon*, or New Year of the Tree. The first-century, B.C.E. master sage Shammai the Elder held it to be at the very first sliver of the Moon of Sh'vaht while his colleague Hillel the Elder held it to occur at the full moon phase of Sh'vaht, the fifteenth day of the month.[1] The consensus eventually followed the opinion of Hillel the Elder, and to this day the Jewish people celebrate the fifteenth day of Sh'vaht, or ט"ו בשבט *tu-besh'vaht*, as a special day commemorating the renewal of the trees. These celebrations range from ritual feasts comprised solely of nuts, dried fruits and fruit juices, to organized communal tree-plantings.

During this special month when we sense the renewal of the living pulse of Tree, we acknowledge its myriad gifts of shelter, shade, beauty and nourishment. The ancients reminded us that the human shares a very special relationship with Tree: "The life force of the human emanates solely from the tree," they taught.[2] The Torah describes the human as akin "to the tree of the field."[3] Cutting down trees is frowned upon by Judaism unless it is absolutely necessary, and this does not mean clearing land for the purpose of development: "It happened that a man tore up his orchard when a fierce wind came and wounded him."[4] Nor would such a venture prove profitable, as "one who cuts down healthy trees shall see no blessing in their lifetime."[5] Trees, the ancient rabbis taught, "communicate with one another and with all of the Creations."[6] It therefore follows that "when a healthy tree is cut down, its groan is heard from one end of the universe to the other."[7]

The particular attribute of this moon has to do with Taste, with flavor, which implies the act of lending meaning and purpose to one's actions and choices in life. This quality has a lot to do with creativity as well, since we need to be quite creative to bring meaning and purpose to our lives, to bring spice, flavor, color, texture, to the course that we choose to take. The ancient teachers remind us that the Torah tells us what we can and cannot eat, but not how to prepare it, or with what to flavor it. That remains our choice.[8]

Of the twelve tribes of Israel, the moon of Sh'vaht corresponds to the tribal archetype of Joseph. Joseph — or יוסף *yo'sef* in Hebrew — literally means "Shall increase." His mother, the matriarch רחל Rachel, named him so as a declaration of faith, that this boy, her first biological child after many years of infertility, will *increase* her fertility and bounty. Eventually Joseph himself continuously "increases" — evolves — and ends up as second to the Pharaoh, and is assigned by the Pharaoh to plan for a major seven-year famine. In spite of the famine, Joseph's skillful planning enables Egypt to become bountiful and sufficiently supplied throughout those seven years with enough grain to feed people across Egypt as well as starving stragglers from other lands.

Joseph is blessed with the fortitude of his mother, Rachel, who although she was unable to get pregnant for many years, did not see her miraculous birthing of Joseph as an anomaly, a once-in-a-lifetime occurrence never again to be repeated. Rather, Rachel seized the gift of the unusual phenomenon of her son's birth and declared it part of a *continuum*. And she called him: "Shall Increase," as in Shall Continue. Her declaration went like this: "God will further gift me with another child."[9] And sure enough she soon gave birth thereafter to Jacob's very youngest, בנימין Binyamin.

Joseph was a dreamer, a visionary, who never stopped believing in his own interpretation of his own dreams. He trusted the process, even when at first life did not unfold for him quite as he had expected. First, he ended up being dumped into a pit by his jealous brothers,[10] then he was sold to some Bedouins who in turn sold him into slavery in Egypt.[11] Next, he is thrown into prison for a crime he did not commit.[12] Yet, *not once* during all of these harrowing episodes of his life did he throw up his arms and abandon hope. *Not once* during all of these graduating series of unfortunate events did he give up on his dreams. *Not once* did he fall into the pits of disappointment and abandon his understanding of the meaning of his dreams that one day he would be on top and his brothers would come bowing to him. And eventually that is exactly what happened. It was not something he had necessarily wished for; it was an actual series of dreams he had, and he believed in them.

Sh'vaht therefore is an auspicious month for drawing forth creative ways of adding flavor to our life processes, and reminds us to never give up hope and never abandon our dreams. "Even if the sword is at your neck," taught the first-century sage, Avee Abba, "do not despair of hope."[13]

Joseph was part of an extended family involving an aging father, four mothers, eleven brothers, and one sister. He was next to the youngest in this family. He was the favorite of his very old father, Jacob, and a source of discord amongst his elder brothers who saw him as favored and arrogant. His brothers saw him this way because he was always bragging to them about his dreams that one day they would recognize his greatness, and even come prostrating before him. In the end, his brothers came to realize that he wasn't actually being arrogant in sharing his dreams with them. They realized that he was simply sharing a vision he had of his future, a vision that had been gifted to him from God, as in prophecy, and they eventually acknowledged him for who he was rather than for who they *presumed* he was. Aware of their shame, Joseph tries to console them, to make them feel okay about themselves and not allow what they did to him to linger and create conflict amongst themselves. He reassures them that all of it was part of the great Divine plan — a*ll* of it — even his being sold into slavery because of them.[14]

Joseph was revered by Hebrew and Egyptian alike until the day he died. Until his last breath he never let go of his vision, of his teaching and staunch belief in Hope. Before his death, he sensed the change that was looming overhead in the climate of Egypt. A new regime was moving in and the Jews would not be treated too well. And so, with his last breath he assured his people of future hope no matter how grim the immediate future appeared. "One day," he said, "God will redeem you from this place; swear to me that you will take my bones along with you."[15] And our ancestors did just that, they remembered to take his bones with them when they left Egypt,[16] which also means that for those 210 years during which they were slaves in Egypt, they clung tenaciously to that very hope of redemption that Joseph left them with.

Joseph's tribes, descendants of his two sons Efrayim and Menasheh, were positioned in the West during the desert journey.[17] West in Hebrew is מערב *ma'arav*, which implies "Blending," as in the blending of light and darkness, day and night, dream and realization, faith in the presence for what is hoped for in the future. West is where the sun sets, which is described throughout the Hebrew Scriptures as בא השמש *bo ha'shemesh* "*coming* of the Sun"[18] when one would suppose it ought to be "*going* of the Sun." The ancient Biblical Hebrew vocabulary has no such word as "Sunset" or "Sundown." In later periods, we began to use the word שקיעה *sh'key'ah* — "sinking" — as in "sinking of Sun," but you will not find any like term used throughout the more ancient vocabulary of the Jewish people. Because in the Hebrew mindset, the Sun never actually goes down. It is always *coming*. You just have to wait it out, for ultimately the Sun will be coming, always coming, never going, never setting, never leaving. It is this mindset that helped Joseph remain steadfast in his faith that in the end all will be well. He always believed, always knew, that the Sun is coming, that daylight will emerge again for him and redeem him from the darkness.

The Totem of the tribe of Joseph, and thereby also of the moon of Sh'vaht is complicated, because the tribe of Joseph was split into two, emerging from his two sons, אפרים Efrayim and מנשה Menasheh. Joseph's *personal* Totem is twofold: the *porat* פורת Wild Donkey[19] and the shor שור Buffalo,[20] which symbolize unwavering tenacity, self-sufficiency and an unbreakable sense of independence.

The Totem for the tribe of Efrayim, who became the primary representative of the Joseph clan, is the שור *shor*, or Buffalo, and that of Menasheh, the ראם *re'aym*, or Oryx, a large and powerful desert-dwelling antelope.[21]

The attribute of Buffalo has to do with family ties and commitment. The Buffalo, according to the Kabbalah, is representative of containment, of the power to slow down unbridled frenzy, and redirect it toward creative and constructive ends. The Buffalo therefore represents הוד *ho'd*, majesty,[22] meaning being in one's full power without necessarily having to exert it or demonstrate it, but simply by one's presence and demeanor, by one's conviction and emotional honesty. Family ties, the Buffalo teaches, are kept snug and secure when the knot isn't too tight, when there is containment in our reaction to family members, rather than impulsive response. "The world is sustained," taught the ancient rabbis, "only in the merit of the one who remains silent in the heat of conflict."[23] Reaction is important, response is often *more* than necessary, it is *imperative*. And so is timing — to pull back and respond or react from a place of clarity, as opposed to a place of impulsivity.

Buffalo teaches us to slow down and channel our power from within our presence, our selfhood, our belief in ourselves, our self-conviction and confidence; to stand our ground with honor and integrity. In moments of discord, where the family or relationship ties become unknotted by conflict, we stand firm and integrate all of the pieces of who we are, get in touch with our own power and greatness, and show our horns — but without goring anyone in the process. Buffalo is then about accomplishing conflict resolution by mere presence, by one's countenance, not by fighting but by being very present in the fullness of one's power, one's stance. Just as Joseph — whose Totem is the Buffalo — overcame the plotting of his brothers and took reign of the rulership of the mighty Egyptian Empire without lifting a finger. He accomplished all this merely by his presence, by integrating all of himself and bringing all of his qualities to the forefront when needed.

The *Wild Donkey* represents independence and freedom. It refuses to carry any weight or to be saddled. Quite often we find that the child of Sh'vaht will conform to a job or commit to a relationship and to all of the responsibilities that go with either, only to shirk all and flee for the hills as her Wild Donkey attribute sets in. The Buffalo quality in the Sh'vaht person will move them toward commitment to family ties and relationships, whereas the Wild Donkey quality may appear as well and move them to evade both. The more aware the child of Sh'vaht is of these archetypal tendencies, the better they are able to dance between their seemingly opposite qualities to forge a more wholesome and powerful quality, such as that of the Totem of Joseph's elder son, Menashe, the ראם *reh'aym*, or Oryx. At times, the child of Sh'vaht may discover that their life direction is best nurtured within the context of relationships, and at times they may realize that they are best nurtured outside any defined context, in the open-ended spaces of chance. In the story of Joseph, his obsession is initially with his family ties. They are the exclusive theme of his dreams and visions. He is pure Buffalo. Yet, he eventually sabotages those ties and ends up in Wild Donkey mode, separated from his family and cast from one wild adventure to another, making no attempt to contact his family even when he rose to become second to the Pharaoh. In the end, he re-unites with his family again, this time as the all-powerful Oryx.

The Oryx, is, again, a large and powerful antelope with very long, very sharp horns, and thrives in the most arid of deserts. And while usually animals who live in the desert are smaller in size due to the lack of foliage and water, the Oryx overcomes the lack of available nourishment of its environment and grows tall and mighty, therefore representing inner strength that we draw from deep within ourselves regardless of what is available to us from outside of us. The Oryx is therefore described in the Torah as an animal of great power. In fact, the Divine power that enabled us to thrive in the most arid of desert regions during our 40-year trek out of Egypt, is described as akin to "the strength of the Oryx."[24] In the Midrash, we find that the ancient sages spoke of the Oryx as symbolic of both the constructive and destructive attributes of the Divine, that there are circumstances or times when God's intervention in the world involves *sustaining* the world, and there are times and circumstances when God's intervention in the world involves what we experience as destruction. Both these seemingly opposite qualities of Divine intervention are symbolized in the Oryx.[25]

The stone that belongs to the moon of Sh'vaht and to the tribes of Joseph, is the שהם *sho'hahm*, the Onyx, a very powerful and paradoxical stone. This stone, the Kabbalah teaches, has the power to calm you if you become delusional and to create delusions if you don't have any (*Sefer Big'dey Kehunah*). It is a dream conjurer, and is therefore very sensitive, and is to be used very sparingly. It also brings about charisma and visions — the qualities of the archetype of Joseph. The onyx is like a medicine. Take too much of it and it harms you. It challenges us to walk between the extremes, to walk in balance, to not over-react. To not take things too far - *anything*. This stone was rarely handled, it was mostly carried by the ancient High Priest of Israel, the *ko'hayn gah'do'l* כהן גדול, sewn into his ceremonial garment and the only stone that decorated his shoulders. It signified that we *carry* our visions, we don't *grasp* them — we don't impose them on others. We *carry* our visions, our charisma, our dreams, *peripherally*, not overtly, not in the palms of our hands and not on our sleeves. If we did so, that would imply that we are endeavoring to control and *direct* our visions rather than allowing them to unfold in their own time at their own pace. The onyx reminds us that when we try to control, direct or force things to happen, we are actually being controlled *by* those events, rather than the other way around.

The onyx stone represents also the qualities of kindness and goodness.[26] The onyx was the only stone that came to the people not from the Earth but from the clouds,[27] the moisture of the kiss of Heaven and Earth, of spirit and matter, of Creator and Creation. It therefore wields forces that can easily represent the qualities of either, depending on the persona of the one who carries it. The thick nature of its blackness can either reflect light in its fullest brilliance, or absorb darkness in its fullest dimness.

The herb for Sh'vaht is מעלה עשן *ma'aleh ah'shahn*, or smoke-rising, a plant that was essential for the sacred incense offering at the altar in ancient Israel. The smoke of the herbal mixture of the incense offering rose up in a perfectly straight, even line from Earth to sky, symbolic of the intent to direct the prayers of the people in a smooth, unwavering stream. This smoke-rising plant enabled this to occur, meaning it conjured the spirits of the plants employed in this mysterious blend, enabling them to transcend and return to the spirit realm in the most harmonious and healing manner. Again, the lesson of balance. Nothing tends to go straight and smooth when we quicken it, when we force it against its own pace and timing, when we act impulsively. Straight and smooth requires presence, balance, majesty, containment, steadfastness and endurance. These are the qualities of integration found in the Wild Donkey, Oryx and Buffalo totems of Joseph.

Ma'aleh a'shahn mediates between sky and Earth, spirit and matter, moving the smoke and aroma of the sacred incense mix to rise and carry Earth into sky in a perfectly straight line. It is about faith in oneself, braving transcendence, and moving oneself toward spirit without anxiety, without looking to the sides to see if one is doing it right, but just doing it with the trust that one is doing it right. In an ancient mode of Jewish shamanic journeying known as *par'des* פרדס, or The Orchard, the participant is warned not to look at anything peripherally, not to "peek" to one side or the other, but to move straight through it, undistracted.[28]

The *ma'aleh a'shahn* herb is not identified. Its identity has been kept secret for thousands of years and was known only to the ancient House of אבטינס Av'tee'nus, a family of *ko'hanim* who were the sole masters of the Sacred Incense in ancient times.[29] The mysterious blend of this smoke-rising herb is unknown to us, gone along with the clan of Av'tee'nus. It is not known in our own times whether anyone has been able to trace their lineage to this family, let alone whether any such remnants of the clan retained the secret of this herbal blend through the millennia. The sole mention of *anything* remaining of this clan is of a chip from the rock wall of one of their homes, which the ancient rabbis believed was taken off to Rome during the invasion of Jerusalem 2,000 years ago.[30] Why a piece of their wall? Probably because it retained some of the aroma of the sacred blend.

The Talmud recounts how the ancient rabbis, wanting to see whether the blend could be duplicated, hired herbal wizards from Alexandria, Egypt, but even they were unable to create a blend that would replicate a perfectly straight, solid stream of unwavering rising smoke "as straight as a stick." When the rabbis asked an elder from the clan why they refused to divulge the secret of their blend, he replied: "For we know that the Holy Temple is destined to be destroyed, and we do not wish others to misuse the ritual of the Sacred Incense in worship which is antithetical to its intent." The second-century Rabbi Akiva recalls an account by his colleague Rabbi Yishma'el ben Lu'ga who was gathering herbs in the field one day alongside a young boy of the family of Av'tee'nus. Suddenly, the boy began to weep, then laugh.

> "Why did you cry?" Rabbi Yishma'el asked him. "I cried because of how the great honor once accorded my ancestors has now diminished [since the fall of the Temple]." Rabbi Yishma'el then asked him: "Well, why did you then laugh?" Replied the boy: "I laughed when I was reminded that the Holy Blessed Source [God] shall one day restore this honor to us in the time to come." Rabbi Yishma'el then asked him: "What reminded you of this?" Said the boy: "The smoke-raiser [plant] told me." Rabbi Yishma'el grew excited. Perhaps the mysterious herbal ingredient of the Sacred Incense would finally be revealed to him. "Show it to me," he pleaded. "Which among these plants is it?" The boy shook his head and said: "We are sworn to secrecy about its identity, so I am not permitted to point it out to anyone, whatsoever."[31]

Finally, around that same period, an elder of the House of Av'tee'nus approached Rabbi Yochanan ben Nuri, a sage he deeply trusted, and handed him an ancient scroll. "This scroll has been handed down from ancestor to ancestor," he told Rabbi Yochanan. "I give it now into your hands, so be very careful with it, for therein are contained the secrets of the Sacred Incense blend."[32] Oral Tradition has it that when he opened up the scroll to show it to the master, Rabbi Akiva, the scroll crumbled into dust, at which point Akiva's son-in-law Ben Azai declared: "They will call you by your name; they will restore you to your place" — meaning, everyone is accorded their distinct uniqueness of which they alone are the Keeper. Any attempt at giving away to others what it is that we are the designated keepers of, is then futile. Joseph tried to reveal to his brothers the meanings of the dreams and visions that were distinctly in his keeping, and suffered the consequences for so much as his *attempt* to do so.

The house of the moon of Sh'vaht, meaning its umbrella quality that houses all of the above, is בית האהבה *Bayt Ha'ahavah, House of Love.* Love cannot be forced. Love needs to be anything but waivering; love requires the quality of the smoke-rising herb. Love requires patience, containment, stepping back from impulsive reaction. Love requires integration, so that when we say "I love you" the "I" blows at us from the Wind of West — *ma'arav* מערב — literally, from the place of blending; a rich blend of all of our parts, all of who we are, of all of our strengths, our weaknesses, our powers and our vulnerabilities. Love, the Torah teaches us, requires your heart, your resources, your very soul.[33]

Love in the Judaic sense is best defined by its Hebrew term, אהבה *ahavah,* which is rooted in the Judeo-Aramaic word הב *Hav. Hav,* in turn, literally translates as "Give." According to the Kabbalah, or Jewish mystery wisdom, this is how the universe was created. Creation resulted from Creator's will to *gift* of Itself to Other. The nature of this gifting involved also the act of stepping back, pulling Self inward in order to enable the existence and flourishing of *Other*. This is known as *tzim'tzum* צמצום — God's act of self-constriction, so to speak, in order to enable the possibility of Other.[34] God thus models for us what love entails, selfless gifting to Other by the dynamics of stepping back to enable the emergence and blossoming of Other.

This is not about making yourself smaller so that someone else can feel bigger. It is not about negating your own worth in order to amplify or heighten someone else's worth. It is rather a gifting to Other in the form of an invitation, an invitation for Other to share in your personal space — and of course within given boundaries. It is the act of expanding your own private world to enable space for another to join *with* you without crowding you by *their* presence and without them feeling crowded by *your* presence, while leaving your distinctiveness in-tact.

The great 18th-century master, Rabbi Dov Ber of Mezeritch taught that love between people happens when each party steps back from their ego needs to create space for the other in their mutual moment of mutual interaction. By so doing, the two connect, and each gifts of themselves to the other, and by such gifting, by such honoring, each receives and experiences from the other what we call Love.[35]

Therefore did the ancient rabbis define *authentic* love as that love which does not hinge on any factor, on any contingency or expectation, because if it does, then once that factor is gone, so is the love.[36] *Romantic* love is different. It *does* have contingencies. It requires compatibility, trust, and mutual nurturance since it involves intimacy. Is romantic love then a step *down* from altruistic love? Not at all. If the intent is pure, so will become the love that is seeded by the romance, and what will then ultimately unfold is unconditional love. *Romantic* love — with all of its ulterior motives — is nonetheless made possible to begin with by contingency-free *altruistic* love that is seeded deep within each of us, which then blends with *self*-love to forge a love that retains both altruistic love and contingency love. Hopefully, with time and with the achievement of the right balance, or the right mix, the *non*-contingency aspect of the love looms large enough to override any failures or glitches of the *contingency* aspect of it. In this way, the relationship can eventually graduate from the quality of Contract, the quality of "either/or," to the quality of Covenant, the quality of "no matter what." And of course, we are talking about all this in a context of relationship void of any abuse. We are asked to compromise in relationships to the point of bending, not to the point of breaking.

Even romantic love can then be a *requisite* step into the inner *sanctum* of love, a sampling of the "World to Come," where love is not merely a state of Grace but a state of Bliss. The path to this realm, however, is heavily guarded by innocent-looking yet intimidating כרובים *Cherubim* whirling flaming swords of spiritual fire, daring us to approach and take it all the way, or play it safe and linger *near* the Tree of Life but not dare approach it or touch it. [37]

The paradox of this ancient wisdom around Love is that true or ideal love is achieved not through denial of the contradictory and often bewildering nature of love, but rather in understanding love as a multi-dimensional dance of the soul during our life walk.

This is why the Shadow House, the house *opposite* to Sh'vaht, opposite to Love, is the House of Children, since a parent's love for her child is integral, unconditional, and children themselves come to us with emotional honesty and a lack of inhibition. And, of course, love is what we would hope conceives and births and raises the child. Conversely, the child challenges our even-ness, calls our bluff, disrupts our steadfastness, tests our love, tries our patience, interrupts our romance, and upsets our endurance. The shadow challenges of child energy can come at us from an actual child born of our womb, or the child within, or a student, since the ancient rabbis held that when you teach someone, it is considered as if you have actually given birth to them. [38] The Shadow House for Sh'vaht challenges us to love altruistically, even if our children roll their eyes at our every word, or when they get into mischief that is deeply upsetting. Our nature as parents to love our children no matter what, can help us to also love our partners no matter what — to a degree, of course, absent any emotional or physical abuse. Love and caring of children, as challenging as it may be at times, to giving or receiving love with our relationship partners, can also be important guides toward a deepening of our connection with others. This is important for *anyone* to work at in healing their *inner* child, all the more so for the Sh'vaht child. It will bring greater understanding of self and greater ease in relating with children in general.

The *Zodiac* symbol for the moon of Sh'vaht is the water pitcher, the דלי *d'lee*, a vessel within which is contained the quality, the power, that draws forth dream to realization, potential to fruition: Water.

Buffalo is the keeper of the West, which is the place of the element Earth. Water is the element of the South, where the Human is the keeper. [39] Human and Earth both bear the same name in Hebrew, אדמה *Ahdahmah* for Earth, אדם *ahdahm* for Human. Because both bring forth the deepest potentials of the other. The human seeds the soil and brings forth endless varieties of the Earth's possibilities of expression of vegetation, and the Earth in turn inspires the human with its breathtaking scenery, its color, fragrance and texture, to call forth the possibilities of soul expression, to become creative, to achieve art, poetry, healing, joy, song, and peacefulness. Likewise, the water in the pitcher of Sh'vaht, the water of South, is needed by the Earth in West to open up the seeds of potential that lie buried in the soil. Water in turn needs Earth to help contain it, to create boundary, to direct its flow in ways that nurture.

And let us not forget the Oryx. The transcendent faith of the Oryx conjures water out of thin air, calls forth dormancy to fruition even when the wherewithal to do so is scarce, even where there is a dearth of water, and in settings where Earth yields no fruition.

Understandably, therefore, the letter of the Hebrew alphabet that corresponds to the moon of Sh'vaht is the צ from the word *Tzadeek* צדיק, in Hebrew for — balance, rightness, justice. If you are a child of Sh'vaht, you need to be cautious in these regards, to do your utmost to have clarity in seeing the truth of what is actually justice, actually rightness; to do your best not to be clouded by delusion or by the unbridled frenzy of Wild Donkey without applying the healing of Buffalo to old wounds.

The letter צ is also known as צדי *Tzadee*, which implies a net, as in a fishing net. As a fishing net, צ helps us to captivate and take in the bounty, the gifts of the moment; for to live in balance, we need to avoid losing out on the gifts of the present by obsessing with the unknown future, or lamenting the past. Joseph endeavored to make the very best of every tragic moment in his life, rather than obsessing with the anxiety over his future and worrying about why his dreams were not appearing to materialize. Rather, he was present fully through every phase of his dreams' unfolding, through his being sold, through his being enslaved, through his being framed, and through his being imprisoned. In the end, all of his efforts in making the best of his every moment earned him the very moment he had dreamed about. They earned him the respect of some of his fellow inmates in prison, among which were ministers of the Pharaoh, one of whom would later win him an audience with the Pharaoh himself as an interpreter of Pharaoh's disturbing dreams — and eventually as vice-ruler of the entire land of Egypt.

NOTES

1. *Mishnah, Rosh Hashanah* 1:1.
2. *Midrash Sif'ri, D'varim* 20:19).
3. Deuteronomy 9:25.
4. *Midrash B'reishis Rabbah* 13:2.
5. *Talmud Bav'li, P'sachim* 50b.
6. *Midrash Bereisheet Rabbah* 13:2.
7. *Midrash Pirkei D'Rebbe Eliezer*, Ch. 34.
8. *Talmud Bav'li, Nedarim* 20b.
9. Genesis 30:24.
10. Genesis 37:24.
11. (Genesis 37:28 and 39:1).
12. Genesis 39:20.
13. *Talmud Bav'li, B'rachot* 10a.
14. Genesis 50:19-21.
15. Genesis 50:24-25.
16. Exodus 13:19.
17. Numbers 2:18-19.

18. E.g.,, Genesis 28:11, Exodus 17:12 and 22:25, Leviticus 22:7, Psalms 50:1 and 113:3, Ecclesiastes 1:5, Malachi 1:11, etc.

19. Genesis 49:22.

20. Deuteronomy 33:17.

21. Deuteronomy 33:17.

22. 16th-century Rabbi Moshe Cordovero in *Pardes Rimonim*, 1:1.

23. *Talmud Bav'li, Chullin* 89a.

24. Numbers 23:22.

25. *Talmud Bav'li, Gittin* 68b; and commentary of the 16th-century Rabbi Yehudah Loew of Prague [MaHaRaL] in *Chidushay AgGahdot,* Part Two, folio 128, *Mesechet Gittin.*

26. 16th-century Rabbi Yehudah Loew of Prague [MaHaRaL] in *Netzach Yisra'el,* Ch. 51, folio 195.

27. *Talmud Bav'li, Yoma* 75a.

28. *Talmud Bav'li, Chagigah* 14b.

29. *Talmud Bav'li, Yoma* 38a.

30. *Talmud Bav'li, Avot D'Rebbe Natan* 41:12.

31. *Talmud Bav'li, Yoma* 38a.

32. *Talmud Bav'li, Tosef'ta Yoma* 2:7.

33. Deuteronomy 6:5.

34. 16th-century Rabbi Chaim Vidal in *Etz Chaim, Heichal Alef, Sha'ar Rishon, Anaf Bet.*

35. *Torat HaMaggid Mi'Mezeritch*, Vol. 1, p. 115.

36. *Mishnah, Avot* 5:16.

37. Genesis 3:24.

38. *Talmud Bav'li, Sanhedrin* 19b.

39. Zohar, Vol. 2, folio 24a; *Midrash Bamid'bar Rabbah* 2:9; see also 13th century Rabbi Yitzchak of Akko in *Sefer M'irat Einayim, Bamidbar*, para. 2.

Chapter Thirteen

Adar

(February 11–March 28, and January 31–March 10 in Leap Years)

Adar אדר, meaning "Glory" and "Honor"

Attribute: Laughter צחוק *tse'cho'k*, and Playfulness, שחוק *s'cho'k*

Tribe: Bin'yamin, בנימין *Bin'yamin* meaning "Son of Rightness"

Tribal Totem: Wolf זאב *z'ev* with the quality of loyalty and individuality

Tribal Stone: Jasper ישפה *yish'pah* with the quality of calming and communication

Tribal Herb: Cinnamon קינמון *kee'nah'mo'n*

House: Enmity בית האיבה *bayt ha'ay'vah*

Zodiac: Fish דג *dahg*

Letter: *ku'f* ק Monkey

Tribal Flag: צילוב כל הצבאים Blend of all [11] Colors *tzee'loov kol hat-ze'va'im*, with image of a wolf

Tribal Direction: West, מערב *ma'arav*, "Blending"

Adar אדר literally means "Glory" and "Honor," as it is a month all to itself, neither of Winter nor of Spring. It is the last of the months on the Hebrew calendar, the finale, the moon of limbo; no longer Winter, not yet Spring. It is the "And," the linking moon that links the bareness of Winter to the fruition of Spring, the Omega to the Alpha, the very end to the very beginning — where the tail of the snake finally reaches the mouth of the snake, the month of Nee'sahn, which is the first of the months on the Hebrew calendar. Snake in Hebrew is *nachash* נחש, which also translates as Trickster. Adar is when the Trickster comes full circle and if we haven't learned anything from the

111

challenges he has brought us until now, they will stop and start anew in different shapes and venues.

Adar is the month of wait-and-see, where we hold our breaths to see whether Winter has swallowed up all potential for the furtherance of Life, or whether Winter has, during all these dark moons, been busily germinating and nourishing the seeds we planted in Autumn, preparing them for re-emergence in Spring. Adar is then the doorway to new beginnings, to the first of the months, Nee'sahn, which is the moon of Wonder, of Miracle. As a bridging month linking Winter's dormancy to Spring's fruition, it is about distinction and separateness, both secondary meanings to the Hebrew word *adar* אדר.

Adar is a very auspicious moon for our people. It is the month in which Moses was born and the month in which he died — both occurring on the seventh day of Adar.[1] It is also the month in which the entire Jewish people worldwide were scheduled for total annihilation by the cruel degree of Haman, and the month in which that very decree was overturned by the actions of Queen Esther.[2] Birth and death, apocalypse and turnabout, the linkage of both, the simultaneous embrace of both, a theme dramatized in the time of Passover through the hands-on ritual of smearing blood on both sides of our doorposts.[3] The blood on both sides of the doorposts represents life and death, both of which sit on either side of the passageway of transformation through which we boldly step into our exodus. And they are unified by the oneness of both as symbolized by the blood on the cross-beam that unites both sides of the passageway.

Adar is therefore a month of coming full circle, a month of completion. And completion happens best in limbo, in between, in the chasm between past and future; in the mystery of the elusive moment between moments, the space of non-space. It is the simple point of both beginning and end, where the primal thought and its final actualization rejoin each other. The climax of an action, wrote the 14th-century Rabbi Shlomo Alkabetz, resides in the original thought that ultimately led to that action."[4]

Moses, like Esther, is a reluctant prophet, hesitating at the doorstep of uncertainty, at the brink, the very edge overlooking the fathomless cauldron of the Abyss, swirling with the forces of Genesis and Nemesis. Esther at first argues with her uncle Mordechai's request that she risk entering the chamber of the king to redeem her people.[5] Moses, too, at first argues with God's request that he risk returning to Egypt[6] — where he was a wanted man — and convince the Pharaoh to redeem his people. Both finally step boldly into danger — Esther at the pain of death for violating the king's edict that no one dare enter his space without being summoned, and Moses who, no sooner does he set out on his journey toward Egypt, is nearly killed by an obstructive Spirit.[7]

Both Esther and Moses wreak havoc on their adversaries, turning everything upside down and inside out, Moses in Egypt, Esther in Persia. Both guide the people in the science of exile and survival in a strange land — Esther teaching us how to find God and Miracle in exile, and Moses teaching us how to find God and Miracle in the middle of the wilderness, far from the homeland. And both renew the strength and backbone of the people and usher them into a completely new paradigm. Finally, both Esther and Moses conceal their identity as Hebrews prior to their being compelled out of the closet and into their respective prophetic missions.[8] In both scenarios, that of Esther and that of Moses, the attribute of the Hebrew moon of Adar is played out through the quality of hesitation, concealment, waiting for the right moment-between-moments to emerge into revelation and fruition.

Adar is then the limbo moon during which we wait with bated breath and hesitant hope, and trust that what had been concealed in the previous moons of Winter will become revealed once again in the forthcoming moons of Spring. Somewhat like a gamble, a lottery. It is then not coincidental that in Adar we celebrate the festival we call פורים Purim, which literally means "lotteries" as in chances.[9] Because it was in the month of Adar about 2,500 years ago that our adversary at the time, Haman, cast a lottery to pick a date on which he would have the Jewish people completely annihilated across the entire empire of Persia, which at the time stretched from India to Ethiopia.[10] The day picked in this lottery, in this *purim*, was the 13th day of Adar.[11] In the end, however, the entire episode was turned on its head, and the 13th day of Adar became a day the Jews were empowered to pre-empt the tragic plan for their genocide and overcome those who sought their doom.[12] We do not celebrate Purim on the day commemorating the tragedy of having to kill our enemies, but on the following day, on the 14th of Adar, in respect to the ancestral teaching: "Do not rejoice at the fall of your enemy."[13]

The 13th of Adar is then a very auspicious time. It holds within it both the seemingly overwhelming shadow of great challenge, and the empowerment to turn that challenge on its head and overcome it. The celebration of the *festival* of Purim is therefore a ritual venue for readying ourselves for the unknown, the uncertain; for stirring within us the courage and faith we need to move into the next paradigm. And so, on Adar, we commemorate Moses, whose birth and death both occurred in this deeply mysterious moon, and whose life journey, like Esther, was challenged with concealment and emergence, mystery and revelation.

This is the deeper meaning of the translation of Adar, "Glory," as in "the Earth is filled with the Glory of God"[14] — in other words, the splendor of the Divine Presence is both revealed and concealed;[15] you can feel it, see it, sense it, but you cannot quite touch it. Adar therefore also is related to the word used to describe the miraculous spirit-endowed Mantle of Glory worn by Elijah the Prophet — the *Adeh'reht* אדרת.[16] This is the month during which the Earth dons the Mantle of Glory to conjure forth the beginnings of the miracle that will ensue in the Moon of Spring. As such, Adar is the magic wand that touches Winter and magically melts away the snows and the frozen Earth in preparation for Spring.

The attribute for Adar is Laughter, Playfulness — *s'cho'k* שחוק in Hebrew. Because it is laughter and playfulness that melts what has grown cold and softens what has become hard. Of course, laughter, like any other reaction, has its downside as well, such as laughing *at* someone, or being laughed at, laughter in the sense of belittling or mocking. Laughter in the context of joy, however, is a sacred attribute lauded and encouraged throughout the ancient Jewish teachings which held joy as a prerequisite to wholesome spiritual practice and awareness.[17] In fact, the Torah even goes so far as to include the *absence* of joy in spiritual practice as among factors potentially capable of bringing on harsh karmic consequences.[18] Observance of the Torah, the ancients taught, cannot be adequately accomplished without joy.[19] Even the Ten Commandments, they taught, were transmitted "in a language of joy."[20]

Laughter is also an effective way of dissipating conflict. There is a story in the Talmud that goes like this:

> One day, Rabbi B'roka of Chaza'ah was wandering about the marketplace in Lepet when the spirit of Elijah appeared to him. Said the rabbi: "Tell me, is there anyone in this marketplace who is great enough to merit a share in the World to Come?" Said Elijah: "Not a one." As they were walking, they spotted two men in the distance. Said Elijah: "These two are children of the World to Come."
>
> Curious, Rabbi B'roka approached the two and asked them: "What is your work?" Said they: "We are clowns. We cheer up those who are sad. Also, when we see two people in conflict, we intervene and make fun until they become peaceful with one another."[21]

The ancient rabbis were known for their sense of humor and their use of joking and silliness for the purpose of rendering their teachings more "user-friendly." Some teachers even went as far as considering clowning around *essential* for accessing wisdom! And that without the quality of laughter and silliness, they taught, there really *isn't* any wisdom. In the Zohar, one of our most prolific collections of ancient and early medieval Kabbalah, we read the following:

> From jesting, purpose is brought to wisdom, for if there were no silliness in the world, neither would there be wisdom in the world. Indeed, it is a responsibility upon every person to experience a bit of jesting and to know her. For there is a greater purpose lent to wisdom that comes from clowning around as there is greater illumination lent to light that comes from out of the darkness. For without darkness, there is no light, and the light would serve no purpose. For

Rabbi Shim'on once said to Rabbi Abba: "Come and see! The mystery of a thing is not illuminated except within the context of jesting, which awakens it from the other dimension, and if not for that illumination, there would be no empowerment or purpose to wisdom. And the more jesting, the more clarity is brought to wisdom. Moreover, if there would be no jesting found in the world, there would be no wisdom found in the world." And thus did the Grandfather, Rabbi Ham'muna, always begin his mystery teachings for the clan with several jokes, for through jesting does wisdom retain purpose.[22]

On a mystical level, joy and laughter are the result of the exchange of the forces of Water for those of Fire, and vice-versa, the dynamics of opposing elements weaving in and through one another in harmony, each taking on the quality of the other as opposed to dissolving it or extinguishing it.[23] In other words, laughter stems from the celebration of the mystery of paradox and contradiction. We see this in everyday joke-telling, as laughter is triggered by one expectation being exchanged for another. Adar, more than any other moon, carries this quality, the quality of turnabout, paradox, the exchange of opposites, as we see in the story of Purim which is celebrated in Adar in commemoration of just such an event that occurred in Adar.

The tribal archetype that corresponds to Adar is Bin'yamin בנימין which translates as "son of my right hand," so re-named by his father Ya'akov after his mother Rachel had named him בן אוני Ben'o'nee, "son of my suffering." He is the only one of the thirteen children of Jacob who is named by his father. All the others were named by their mothers as was our custom in ancient times. His mother, Ra'chel, died as he emerged from her womb, which prompted her to call him "son of my suffering." But his father, Jacob, quickly renamed him so that the negative connotation of his maternal name would not affect him. He named him according to how he felt toward his dying wife, "son of my right hand,"[24] as Rachel and he were so close she was like his right hand. The archetype of Benjamin reflects the connotations of both names and the intentions behind them: suffering and redemption, failure and triumph. Later, some of his descendants deviated from the morality of the other tribes and adopted some very abusive practices from neighboring cultures, resulting in a costly intertribal war that nearly wiped out the entire tribe of Benjamin altogether.[25]

The first chieftain of all the tribes of Israel — Sha'ul — came from the tribe of Benjamin. He failed abysmally. This archetype could then seem to be about failure. Yet, Benjamin made an incredible comeback through the heroic acts of Esther and Mordechai, two Benjaminites who in the 5th century B.C.E. rescued the entire Jewish population from total annihilation, as we see in the story of Purim. In the end, the lone wolf, the Totem of Benjamin, returns to rescue the entire pack and reintegrates itself into the family of the tribes. Benjamin teaches us that it is never too late. Never. Regardless of your past. You can transform any situation, from suffering to ecstasy, from sadness to joy, from hopelessness to faith, from failure to success.

The Totem of the tribe of Bin'yamin, as we just mentioned, is the Wolf, *z'ev* זאב which in this tradition is about nurturance. [26] Wolf also carries other qualities, such as loyalty and individuality, preserving one's unique selfhood, one's individuality, while also relating to and caring for the family or community. Wolf is the keeper of moon medicine, of the gift that moon brings to us, to the Earth, in each of its phases of unfolding, of waxing and waning. And wolf calls to it, sings to it, knows when to welcome which moon gift for which phase.

The wolf represents family loyalty and also seclusiveness, separateness, as the wolf fluctuates between connection with the pack and wandering off on its own. In the stories around the tribe of Bin'yamin, we find this trait quite dramatically played out. At times the tribe is integrated within the nation of Israel and at times Bin'yamin wanders off on his own, adopting an attitude and mindset quite antithetical to the ways of the other tribes.

Bin'yamin is the youngest child in this large tribal family, and very little is known about him, told about him, in the story. He is — like the wolf — a loner, misunderstood, underestimated, and draws very little attention if any until he sets himself up as a huge thorn that pierces the heart of the nation and draws the other tribes to actually go to war against him, at a huge cost to them of tens of thousands of lives - the power of the youngest turning out to be far greater than all the other eleven tribes combined! Eventually, he is overcome by his brothers and absorbed into the nation once more where he continued to flourish with the pack once again. [27]

The particular birth stone for the moon of Adar — corresponding to the stone that represented the tribe of Bin'yamin on the priestly breastplate — is the Jasper Stone — *Yahsh'pa* ישפה — known to strengthen vision, to alleviate digestive problems, and also known to be helpful for a woman who is experiencing difficulty in labor. The Jasper stone is also known for its medicinal capacity to slow down blood flow, as in lowering blood pressure, or to slow down bleeding. At the same time, though, it also has the risk of decreasing sexual appetite, since it affects the blood flow, subduing passion.

Even though Bin'yamin's mother dies in giving birth to him, his tribal stone has the opposite quality of *helping* a woman in labor. Because the moon of Adar, being the transitional moon from Winter to spring, is therefore also the moon of Turnabout, of turning what is to what is not, or what is not to what is. Again, this is just like the Purim story, which is celebrated in Adar. In addition, the tribe of Bin'yamin were positioned in the West during the exodus journey across the Sinai Desert. [28] And West in our tradition is about blending — *ma'arav* מערב in Hebrew, from the word *l'ah'reyv* לערב, to blend — unifying diversity, as day blends into night in the West, light into darkness, birth into death. In the Jewish tradition, night is the beginning of the next day, and darkness is where the light is concealed until it is time to re-emerge, and death is but the vestibule leading to rebirth.[29]

The moon of Adar is the final moon in the Hebraic calendar just like Bin'yamin is the final son born to Ya'akov. It is the finale before whole new beginnings, before the new counting of the moons begin again, with Nee'sahn, with Spring, with Passover. It is the climax of Winter, of the season of mystery, where what was hidden becomes revealed. Accordingly, we read in Adar *Megilat Ester* מגילה — the Scroll of Esther. *Megilat Esther* also translates literally as "the unraveling of the hidden" — מגילה *megilah* from the word *leh'gah'lo't* לגלות, to unravel — and *es'ter*, אסתר from the word *leh'hahs'teer*, להסתיר to conceal.

The particular plant or herb of the ancient sacred incense that corresponds to Adar and the tribe of Bin'yamin is Cinnamon, or in Hebrew *kee'nah'mo'n* קינמון which implies "acquires much." It is about taking onto yourself the gift of the moment and integrating it with other qualities you walk with in your life. It is about not only receiving and taking in the blessings of life but also combining them, unifying them so that these gifts are not fragmented or compartmentalized but that they rather enhance and enrich each other. As such, this herb has the gift of enabling the other herbs in the incense offering to blend more aromatically, so in a way this herb acquires much, that is, it absorbs the others, unifies them — related to the direction the tribe of Bin'yamin were positioned in the desert, West, place of blending.

Interestingly enough, Bin'yamin unifies the other tribes in two dramatic events, one *for* him, one *against* him. In the story of Joseph in Egypt, Joseph toys with his brothers when they come to him for food without knowing who he was. He then demands that they bring their youngest brother Bin'yamin to him, a risky task that unites the clan and brings them to a uniform acknowledgment of the wrong they had done to their brother Joseph earlier. Centuries later, when the clan of the twelve brothers had morphed into tribes settling the Land of Canaan, a tragic crime occurs among the tribe of Bin'yamin, as mentioned earlier, and Bin'yamin's refusal to extricate the evil that was committed unites the tribes in waging war against him.

The house quality of Adar, of Bin'yamin's spirit realm, is *bayt ha'ay'vah* בית האיבה, or *House of Opposition*, or literally: Enmity. Like the story of Purim, Adar is an arena for the dance of opposites. What Haman plots against the Jewish nation in the story is turned completely around and against him in the end. Traditionally, Jews celebrate this holiday by masquerading themselves as opposites, women as men, men as women, the saintly as villains, etc. In this month we turn solemnity into joy, grieving into dancing,[30] anxiety over what will or will not emerge from the land in the subsequent month of Spring — into celebration; laughing in the faces of adversaries, the obstacles, the doubt, the uncertainty, the unknown.

Adar is not about *struggling* with opposition; it is about *dancing* with it, transforming it, facing it with faith, faith in the process, faith in it being *part* of our life walk, not its antithesis. Like the eighteenth-century Rebbe Nachmon of Breslav taught: "When you are engaged in joyful dance, do not leave your troubles at the door, but rather invite them into the dance so that you might transform them."[31]

The Shadow Moon to Adar, is the month of Elul, whose house is the House of Illness, *Bayt Ha'Cho'lee* בית החולי, the complete opposite of the healing attribute of West, mentioned earlier, and seemingly opposite to all the laughing and dancing, which Adar is supposed to conjure within us. This is because illness can sometimes result from, or be fed by, the opposite of joy. Sadness, depression, grief, tend to weaken our immune system, while joy and song drive away sadness and strengthen our immune system and bring us healing.[32] It is noteworthy that the word for dance in Hebrew is the same as the word for illness: illness is *machalah* מחלה, and dance is *machol* מחול — "for it is through dance," Rebbe Nachmon taught, "that one heals."[33]

The Zodiac for this moon in the Hebrew reckoning is the דג *dahg*, the fish. Fish is representative of other-worldiness, since fish live and breathe in a universe in which none of us could survive for more than a few minutes. Traditionally, this is why Jews tend to eat fish on the Sabbath, as the Sabbath is a "taste" of the World to Come, of other-worldliness.[34] Fish are the creatures of the waters, the primal element from which the Earth and all of her creatures emerged. In the beginning, our creation story tells us, there was only water, and Creator had the water recede to enable the emergence of land.[35] Just like Adar introduces the emergence of the fruits of the land, of Spring.

The Hebrew letter associated with Adar is the letter *kuf* ק, which translates as "monkey" or "ape" — *ko'f* קוף. Just as Adar is almost Spring but not quite, so is monkey almost human but not quite. Monkey represents the wild, uninhibited part of us that is unafraid to act out what we feel in its most primal form, something that Purim celebrations have traditionally encouraged. Monkey is about shedding the definitions that have been imposed on us all year long, in preparation for fresh liberation of our Selfhood in the subsequent month of Nee'sahn and its celebration of Passover. This is an important component of preparing oneself for liberation, by removing the layers that others have placed upon us, or that have been cast before us by life situations. It is about tuning into our spirit selves, our souls.

This is a very auspicious time, the link of what was to what is about to emerge anew. Walk it carefully.

NOTES

1. *Talmud Bav'li, Kidushin* 38a.

2. Esther 9:22.
3. Exodus 12:7.
4. Sabbath Eve Hymn *Lecha Dodee*, second stanza.
5. Esther 4:5-17.
6. Exodus 4:1.
7. Exodus 4:24 — see Rashi; *Talmud Bav'li, Nedarim* 32a.
8. Esther 2:10 and Exodus 2:19.
9. Esther 9:26.
10. Esther 1:1.
11. Esther 3:13.
12. Esther 9:1.
13. Proverbs of Solomon 24:17.
14. Isaiah 6:3.
15. Zohar, Vol. 1, folio 64b.
16. Second Kings 2:13.
17. *Midrash Tanna D'Bei Elyahu Zutta,* Ch. 17.
18. Deuteronomy 28:47.
19. *Midrash Vayikra Rabbah* 34:9.
20. *Midrash Tanna D'Bei Eliyahu Rabbah*, 14:11.
21. *Talmud Bav'li, Ta'anit* 22a.
22. *Zohar*, Volume 3, Folio 47b.
23. Zohar, Vol. 1, folio 103b.
24. Genesis 35:18.
25. Judges, Chapters 20-21.
26. *Midrash Tehilim* 10:13 and 17:14.
27. Judges, Chapters 20-21.
28. Numbers 2:22.
29. 3rd-century Rabbi Ya'akov, quoted in *Mishnah, Avot* 4:16.
30. Esther 9:22; Psalms 30:12.
31. *Likutei MoHaRaN Tanina*, Chapter 23.
32. Isaiah 35:10 and 51:11.
33. *Likutei MoHaRaN Tanina*, Chapter 23.
34. *Talmud Bav'li, Berachot* 57b.
35. Genesis 1:9.

Chapter Fourteen

Second Adar

(March 2–April 8 in Leap Years)

Second Adar — *Adar Shay'nee* — אדר שני (leap year moon), "Glory"
Attribute: Faith אמונה *eh'moo'nah*
Tribe: Deenah, דינה meaning Rightness, Justice, Judgment
Tribal Totem: The Great Sea Dragon (דרקון הים *dera'kon ha'yahm*); Levi-
    athan לויתן *levee'yah'tan*: playfulness and the forces of nature
Tribal Stone: Gold זהב *za'hav* with the quality of perfection
Tribal Herb: Palm Branch לולב *lu'lav*
House: Upheaval ההפכה *bayt ha'ha'fa'chah*
Zodiac: North Star כוכב הצפונה *ko'chav ha'tza'fo'nah*
Letter: *alef* א Chief
Tribal Flag: זהב צהוב Gold Yellow *za'hav tza'hu'v*, with the image of a sea
    dragon
Tribal Direction: Within, פנימה *pe'nee'mah,* "Facing Toward Whatever
    Is"

אדר שני Second Adar is the month that is added onto the Hebraic calendar
every several years to make sure that the first month, Nee'sahn, whose rites
include first-grain-crop offerings, falls in the actual season of the "renewal of
the grain crop," or חדש האביב *cho'desh ha'aveev*, also known as Moon of
Spring. As a people, we began the counting of our months from the time we
were liberated from slavery in Egypt about 3,300 years ago, which occurred
in the month of the "renewal of the grain crop."[1] Grain and other Earth gifts
are of course under the influence of the *solar* cycle, and it is therefore
important that the month of Nee'sahn, the first of the months and which

121

incorporates grain-related ceremonies, *always* coincide with the period during which the Sun brings on the season of Spring, the season of the first
grains. Since the lunar cycle has less days than the solar cycle per annum,
Nee'sahn would inevitably end up way back in Winter, not a season for the
grain crops. Therefore, every several years, when the lunar cycle falls close
to a month's worth of days behind the solar cycle, we add an additional
month to the last month, Adar, and call it Second Adar, or *Adar Shay'nee* אדר
שני.

The attribute of Second Adar is Faith. Faith is about trusting that what is
needed or hoped for will arrive at the time that is most ripe for its appear-
ance. When we trust the process and give God the space, so to speak, to make
things happen at God's pace of determination rather than our own, the response is "timely" and therefore imbued with Blessing as well.[2] What we ask
for in life, or yearn for, may not come to us in the exact form and moment
that we want. Faith means that we trust God has heard us, knows of our
longings, and has already responded, albeit in God's way, and that sometimes the manifestation of that response is akin to a time-release capsule,
waiting for just the right moment and circumstance for its most optimum
realization: "And it shall come to pass, that before they have even called, I
will have answered; while they are still [praying], I will already have
heard."[3] Likewise, Second Adar arrives when it is needed, when it is called
for, to intervene when the Moon of Nee'sahn seems to be slipping away and
in danger of losing its momentum and significance as the pivotal point of all
the other months and their respective seasonal celebrations.

This periodic "Thirteenth Moon" would correspond to the thirteenth
member of the Hebrew ancestral tribal family: Deenah דינה. Deenah was born
to Jacob and Ley'ah. Some traditions have it that she was Jacob's only
daughter, while other traditions have it that there were twelve additional
daughters, as is written: "And all of his sons and all of his daughters rose to
console him [Jacob]"[4] — each born as a twin to each of the twelve sons of
Jacob — and that the brothers and sisters married one another, which was not
forbidden in Jewish law prior to the receiving of the Torah at Sinai.[5]

Like her mother Ley'ah, Deenah is not one to remain confined in any one
place but craves new adventures. She goes out, as the story describes her[6] —
out of her element, out of her status-quo — to see what the world is like
outside the narrow confines of her immediate social and cultural environment. She dares to move within and beyond the tribes, weaving her thread of
mobility and surprise, of challenge and newness, throwing everyone off their
flow and creating havoc.

No matter what the cost, even to herself, she dares to cross the boundaries
set for her by others and forge ever-flexible, elastic pathways which in turn
pioneer fresh encounters for all who encounter her along the way. Just as we
ready ourselves for Passover in the month of Adar, which precedes Nee'sahn,

along comes Deenah and interrupts our calculations and expectations with yet another *additional* moon, a month of *more* laughter and dance, of more celebration of life and hope.

Like her mother, Deenah is drawn toward the feminine forces of life, which took her mother six births to arrive at. Ever since she married Jacob, who was also married to her sister Rachel, Ley'ah competed for his attention. Jacob preferred Rachel, and Ley'ah constantly went after her husband's favor. She named her first two sons after her agony around this, but by the time she had her sixth son, she became elated, and felt that her struggles around her issue with Jacob was over. "God has apportioned me a good portion," she declared. "Now, perhaps, my man will make a home with me."[7] So she is still hoping in the back of her mind that Jacob will one day be as intimately in love with her as he is with her sister Rachel, but, hopes and dreams notwithstanding, she maintains as well her independence of Jacob to preserve her happiness. She says, "God has given me a good portion," meaning it is a gift she claims for herself, independent of her connection to Jacob, or of her hopes for their relationship. Having separated her sense of gift and joy in life from dependence upon her man, she moves deeper and deeper into the power of the feminine, and shortly afterwards gives birth to a girl, Deenah.[8] The archetype of Deenah, the elusive and mysterious thirteenth tribe, will be revealed to us in the World to Come. She is the life force that streams, dances, and slithers through all twelve tribal archetypes, threading them into a single weave, as we shall see. Without her, the twelve splinter into disassociated fragments.

Deenah stems from the Hebrew word for judgment *deen* דין, discernment, differentiation, the capacity to distinguish, to individuate; to see clearly each in their own right. Born with the attribute of discernment, Deenah embraces the feminine, and, like her mother, balances it with the masculine. In fact, our oral tradition tells us that she was actually *male* while inside Ley'ah's womb but was born female. The Talmud notes that right after Ley'ah gives birth to Deenah, her sister Rachel — who had been infertile all this time — suddenly becomes capable of conceiving, and becomes pregnant with her first child, Joseph. Coincidence? Well, the ancient rabbis tell us that when Ley'ah was pregnant with her seventh, she prayed to God on behalf of her sister, arguing that "I have given birth to six sons and am now pregnant with a seventh. Our two hand-maidens have birthed two sons each, and Rachel has birthed *none*. If I am now pregnant with a male child, that would bring the realization of the prophecy of twelve tribal patriarchs into my hands and the hands of our hand-maidens. What of my *sister*? Shall she have no role in this at *all*, or one less than even our hand-maidens?" And so God had compassion on Rachel and "opened her womb" as the Torah tells us[9] so that she gave birth to two of the tribal fathers, Joseph and Benjamin. As for Ley'ah's unborn child, it was in that moment of her prayer transformed from male to female, and became

Deenah. And this is also why Ley'ah named her Deenah, "for she summoned God to *judgment*" over her sister's infertility.[10]

It is no wonder, then, that tradition has Joseph marrying Deenah's daughter אסנת As'naht.[11] After all, his birth was made possible through the prayer of Ley'ah when she was pregnant with Deenah.

But the story of Deenah is not all roses. There are thorns, too. When she wanders out to see what the people of nearby Sh'chehm are like, she is seized by Sh'chehm son of Cha'mor, prince of the Chee'vites, who is deeply taken by her extraordinary beauty, and he forces her into intimacy. Deenah's brother Shim'on reacts immediately and with urgency along with his brother Ley'vee, destroying Sh'chehm and recovering their sister.[12] His zeal for her honor is so intense that one oral tradition has it that Deenah refused to leave her captors unless Shim'on promised to take care of her from then on, and even marry her.[13] It was the only way she would ever feel safe again after her ordeal. Even though her brother Ley'vee was also involved in her rescue, she nevertheless was more drawn to the protective zeal of Shim'on. The third-century Rabbi Aba bar Kahana, however, had a tradition that Deenah eventually married Jo'b.[14]

According to our people's oral tradition, Deenah was impregnated by the prince of Sh'chehm during her ordeal, and that is when she gave birth to Ahs'naht. Because of the stigma that Ahs'naht represented to Deenah's brothers, carrying the genes of Sh'chehm, not to mention his image, and representing the tragic rape of their sister, they had a golden pendant carved for her with the image of a scorpion (representative of Sh'chehm) and engraved with one of the sacred God Names (representative of Deenah). They then hung it around her neck as a protective amulet and sent her on her way. God looked after her and sent the angel Mee'cha'el to guide her to Egypt[15] where she was taken in and adopted by the infertile wife of Potifera, one of the ministers of the Pharaoh. There, she encountered her uncle Joseph who was then a slave in that household. Later, when Joseph would become second to the Pharaoh himself, he would end up marrying Ahs'naht.[16]

The Kabbalah reminds us that there is a spark of the holy kindled even in the soul of a person involved in an evil act, and that this spark will be drawn toward unification with a soul that radiates holiness if and when there is an encounter between the two. Deenah's soul radiated holiness. The prince of Sh'chehm had a *spark* of holiness in his soul that, when he had sex with Deenah, was instantly drawn to the holy qualities of Deenah's soul so that the two created a soul quality that would incarnate more than fifteen centuries later as the famous Talmudic sage Rabbi Chananyah ben Terahd'yon. As is written: "And his soul cleaved within Deenah,"[17] implying that the spark of purity that existed deep within his otherwise tainted soul was drawn to, and became merged with, the holiness it sensed in the soul of Deenah, creating thereby a very holy soul that would one day incarnate as the great second-century sage Rabbi Chananyah ben Terad'yon,[18] father of the famous *female* Talmudic sage, Beruria, who ruled on issues of Jewish law alongside the greatest of the sages of Israel about 1900 years ago.[19]

Ironically, the Kabbalah teaches, we learn from the very evil act of Sh'chehm, during which a spark of his soul merged with the soul of Deenah, three qualities of unification that we ought to seek in our relationship with the *Shechee'nah* שכינה — the feminine face of the Divine. They are: *d'vay'kah, chah'shay'kah,* and *chah'fee'tzah* חפיצה חשיקה דביקה - Bonding, Yearning and Desiring.[20] These three modes, or phases of intimate connection are alluded to in the story itself: "And his soul *bonded* (*va'teed'bahk* ותדבק) within Deenah;"[21] "And Cha'mor spoke with them, saying, 'The soul of Sh'chem my son *yearns* (*chohsh'koh* חשקה) for your daughter;'"[22] and "And the young man did not hesitate to [circumcise himself], for he *desired* (*choh'faytz* חפץ) the daughter of Jacob."[23]

The Zohar points out that the name Deenah דינה, in its Judeo-Aramaic spelling, דינא , juxtaposes into אדני *ah'do'nay*.[24] Ah'do'nay is the substitute pronunciation for the ineffable God Name י-ה-ו-ה YHWH. Moreover, Deenah's mother, Ley'ah, represents on the Earthly plane *Ey'ma Ee'la'ah* אימא עילאה, or Great Mother. She conceived six sons and one daughter, Deenah, who represents the *Shechee'nah* שכינה. The six sons of Ley'ah, of Great Mother, thus represent the six days of the week, and her seventh child, her daughter Deenah, represents the seventh day, the Holy Shabbat.[25]

The bones of all the tribal ancestors were taken to Canaan during the exodus from Egypt,[26] including those of Deenah, which, according to an ancient oral tradition are buried where the second-century, B.C.E. sage, Natai Ha'Ahr'bay'lee was later buried.[27] Natai Ha'Ahr'bay'lee is known for this teaching: "Do not despair from tragedy; do not lose hope because of it."[28] Another tradition has it that Shim'on, Deenah's avenging brother, carried her bones back to Canaan from Egypt long before the period of the Exodus.[29]

The Totem for Deenah is the Great Sea Dragon לויתן *leh'vee'yah'tan,* which is about playfulness and mischief. It is also representative of the elusive and mysterious life force that moves what we call Nature. Leviathan, as it is often called in English renditions, is the great mythic sea dragon who swirls and wallows in the elements — in water, Earth, fire, and wind. At times, the forces of Nature that result from this wallowing and swirling are beautiful and friendly and inspiring, and at times they seem harsh and merciless and destructive.

King David wrote: "You [God] created Leviathan to play with," [30] which, the sixteenth-century Rabbi Yehudah Loew of Prague explains, means that God is intimately and playfully engaged with the Created realms. Leviathan, Rabbi Loew writes, is therefore representative of Creator's very intimate and personal love and desire for Creation — not any particular aspect of it, but *all* of it, cosmically and universally,[31] thus the teaching of the ancients that "the entire world rests on a single fin of Leviathan."³² This love and desire is constricted so that it does not overwhelm Creation, meaning that God holds Itself back from Its own omnipresence, Its fullest expression of Itself in association with Creation, or else Creation would be overwhelmed into oblivion, shatter, implode. This is similar to how we sometimes have to restrain our otherwise overwhelming excitement about something really amazing in order to be able to be with it in a way that does not swallow it up and override everything. In the language of the Kabbalah, we call this process *tzim'tzum* צמצום.

In the metaphoric language of the ancient sages:

> Everything God created, was created masculine and feminine. Likewise, did God create a male Leviathan and a female one; but were they to mate, they would have destroyed the world. God therefore castrated the male and cooked the female, preserving her meat for the future banquet of the righteous.³³

This strange teaching alludes to the mystery of the Feminine, which will not be revealed and fully known until the World to Come that follows the End of Times. It is then, Jeremiah the Prophet wrote, that "God will have created a new phenomenon in the land, for the Feminine will encircle the Masculine,"³⁴ meaning the true power and mystique of the Feminine will arise and have its time to shine. As mentioned in the chapter on the month of Ahv, the second-century Rabbi Shim'on bar Yo'chai taught, that at the beginning of time in the process of Genesis, Creator concealed the power of the Feminine — which is Timing of Expression and Fruition — deep within the Great Void. There, like seed within womb, this force waits for the right timing before emerging to coincide with the need for it within the Created Universe.³⁵

The ancient teachers tell us that the great sea dragon Leviathan represents the dance, the playfulness, of paradox and contradiction, and challenges us when we get bogged down in too much linear thinking, too much logic.³⁶ Leviathan, or in Hebrew — *leh'vee'yah'tahn* לויתן — is actually a play on two words, Borrowed (*lo'veh* לוה) and Shall Be Gifted (*yu'tahn* יתן). It moves us to question at any given moment of our lives whether our lives are on loan or are they gift? Or both? If on loan, we have an awesome responsibility to care for it. If gifted, we can do whatever we please with it. If both, we bear responsibility for our lives, and also retain an equal share in its unfolding, in choosing how we live, as in "living responsibly." Leviathan then hints to us that if we live life humbly and responsibly, as if it were *borrowed*, then it shall be *gifted* to us.

When God told the primeval waters of Creation to gather to one place so that the Earth could emerge into becoming,³⁷ the waters asked God: "Gather *where*? To *what* place?" And God replied: "To the place of Leviathan,"³⁸ which implies that in stepping back to allow Other to manifest, we need to step back not as in belittling ourselves or withdrawing ourselves into invisibility, but rather to shift to a place of playfulness, to the place of Leviathan. Deenah is drawn out of her home by the lure of playfulness, by the songs and musical allurement of the daughters of the village of Sh'chehm.[39] The danger of the Great Sea Dragon is not the allurement as much as allowing ourselves to get caught up in the allurement to the loss of our selfhood. Deenah loses herself by following the allurement all the way into the hands of the prince of Sh'chehm himself, where the joy of playfulness morphs into the tragedy of captivity. There is a huge difference between meandering about in the *place* of the Great Sea Dragon as opposed to the flaming *breath* of the Great Sea Dragon. The breath of the Dragon is destructive, the Midrash tells us, and can only be tempered by the fragrance of the Garden of Eden,[40] meaning: by our remaining connected to our core selfhood. We are to *frolic* in pleasure, joy and play, not to *lose* ourselves *to* it.[41]

In the end of times, the ancients then taught, those who have struggled to maintain the gift of their unique selfhood while also engaged in balanced play in the dangerous arena of Leviathan without being swept up by it, will participate in a grand meal comprised of the flesh of the great Dragon while being sheltered beneath its skin, which shall be for them like a sacred shelter, or *sukkah* סוכה.[42] In other words, if we strive to sail the tumultuous and challenging waves of life without being intimidated by it and giving up, we will succeed in taking our life journey to its highest achievement of spiritual evolution and enlightenment.

An ancient Jewish parable:

> Once it was told to the Great Sea Dragon Leviathan that Fox was the wisest and most clever of all the animals. "Bring me his heart!" demanded Leviathan, "so that I may ingest his wisdom."
> A school of large fish set out immediately for the mission and found Fox scurrying about on the shore. "Fox!" they called. "Come with us! The King of the Sea, Leviathan himself, requests the honor of your presence! He has heard all about your great wisdom and wants to meet you!" Said Fox: "What?! You think I'm crazy? I would drown in an instant if I were to follow you into the sea." The fish replied: "But we would carry you on our backs so that you would not be submerged in the waters, and take you to the place of Leviathan, and he will meet you there without you having to be in the waters deeper than your ankle!"
> Fox thought for a moment: "Hmmmm. It would be a great honor indeed, and there would be no danger involved if they were to carry me on their backs above water." And so Fox climbed on their backs and the fish began to swim out to sea. But soon, Fox began to feel the waves as the fish slowly began to dive under, and he struggled to stay above water, terrified and regretting his decision. His fears were justified moments later when he heard the fish laughing at him as they brought him deeper and deeper into the sea.

"You tricked me!" Fox protested. "Now that you've got me, tell me the truth! What was this really all about?" The fish laughed and shouted: "Leviathan wants to absorb your wisdom by eating your heart! And now we have you!" And they laughed again as they spun him under some more.

Fox did some quick thinking as he sank deeper and deeper into the sea, and yelled, gurgling: "Why didn't you tell me this, to begin with!? It would have been an honor to surrender my heart to the great Leviathan. But alas! I don't usually carry my heart with me. I leave my heart in a safe place whenever I journey away, and only retrieve it when necessary! Take me back to shore immediately, so that I might fetch my heart. Or else you will face severe consequences when you show up without my heart."

The fish stopped laughing and instantly brought Fox up to the surface of the water and swam him back to shore. Once on shore, Fox dropped to the ground laughing so hard he was kicking up his legs and could hardly respond to the puzzled fish. They were growing impatient, waiting for Fox to go fetch his heart. "Fools!" he finally managed to shout at them. "Did you really think any creature can run about without their heart?" And Fox went about his life walk, safe and sound, and the wiser. [43]

Leviathan desires *all* of who we are. Life challenges us constantly to draw out our deepest potentials, luring us into a web of strife, struggle and desperation. This midrashic parable, however, reminds us to not take life too seriously, to not follow that urge to the point of desperation, or else we risk losing our heart, our unique selfhood.

Leviathan, the ancient rabbis taught, was created out of Light and Water in the fifth cycle of Creation. [44] "The entire world," they taught, "rests on a single fin of Leviathan" [45] — representative of the very delicate, fragile balance of living our lives between Light and Water, Light representing the mystery root cause and purpose of our creation, and Water representing how we reflect back that light, what we project back to our creation from our choices and actions.

The stone associated with Deenah and the leap month of Second Adar is Gold — *za'hav* זהב — whose quality is about impregnable perfection. You can melt gold, burn gold, crush gold, but you can never alter gold or destroy it. Gold remains gold, steadily and through any situation. Like its color, it represents light. Not just any light but the Light of Creation, the conduit of the Divine Will connecting Divine Intent with Divine Manifestation. This stone was not worn on the breastplate of the *Ko'hayn Ga'dol* כהן גדול, the High Priest, along with the stones of the other tribes. Rather, it was spread across the sacred implements of the *Mish'kahn* משכן, the sanctuary that our people carried with them from their desert journey into the ancestral homeland, the dwelling place, so to speak, of the Divine Presence.

Gold alone is mentioned by itself over ninety times and across fourteen chapters in the Torah's account of the building of the *Mish'kahn* and the preparation of the priestly vestments and implements. [46] Gold, as representative of the Divine Light concentrated into physical matter, is therefore linked to the Wind of *Tza'fon* צפון, North, the place of Mystery, as it is written in the Book of Job: "From out of the North does Gold emanate, [riding] upon the Divine in awesome splendor."[47] This is why the Cherubim כרובים that adorned the *a'ron ha'b'reet* ארון הברית the Ark of the Covenant from where God spoke to Moshe (Moses), and the Menorah מנורה — whose flames were to burn eternally — had to be made completely of Gold alone.[48]

So sacred is Gold, taught the second-century Rabbi Shim'on bar Lakeesh, that "it was originally not at all intended for use by mortals, if not for the ultimate construction of the *Mish'kahn*."[49] In fact, one Midrash has God taking the blame for the sin of the Golden Calf because God chose to allow Gold to exist in the material realm, even though its power was so potent that it could lead people to worship it: "Who caused this to happen?" God asked, and replied: "I did, for I gave them a great deal of Gold."[50]

Because it is endowed with Divine potency, Gold is associated with transformation, capable of transforming anyone who comes in contact with it, either for better or for worse. It is no wonder, then, that Gold is associated with the first river to emerge from עדן *Ey'den*,[51] the core realm of Divine mystery from which all of Creation flows forth. And that river is named *Pee'sho'n* פישון, literally: Mouth of Transformation: *pee* פ for "mouth of," and *sho'n* שון for "transformation" as in *leh'shah'no't* לשנות "to change."

The sixteenth-century Rabbi Yehudah Loew of Prague considered Gold, which is pure and perfect in itself, as symbolic of the soul, the *neshamah* נשמה, which, too, is pure and perfect in itself[52] — just as it says in that Talmudic prayer that we recite in the morning upon waking: "*Elo'hi, neshamah sheh'nah'tah'tah bee te'horah hee* — היא טהורה בי שנתת נשמה אלהי — My God, the soul that you have gifted within me, she is pure."[53] Gold, taught Rabbi Loew, is very close to the Divine,[54] in that it has the alchemical quality of fostering transformation and is immutable — as mentioned earlier regarding the river *Pee'sho'n* and its association with Gold — and that it is the translator of Creator's will for Creation to become, calling forth manifestation in the material realm.[55] Light represents that which brings dormancy to fruition, he writes, "because when the light is kindled, all that has been concealed becomes manifest, becomes revealed." Gold, then, carries a high form of light concentrated within it, namely Divine Light, which represents the Divine Will that conjured Creation into being, and into becoming.

This is the quality of Second Adar, of Deenah, who remains pure and steadfast through thick and thin, and, for good or bad purposes, draws forth the deepest potentials that lay dormant in the deepest recesses of consciousness. Accordingly, the direction of Deenah is "Within" as she is inherent among all of the tribes. She dwells within each of them as the Feminine Force as we see dramatically played-out with Shim'on and Ley'vee. And even in her tragic encounter with the prince of Sh'chehm, she still manages

to call forth from deep within him the miniscule holy spark that still remained in his soul — that part of his core being that was Gold — calling it
forth so loudly that it merged with her own soul, creating thereby the soul of
the future sage Rabbi Chanan'yah ben Terahd'yon.

The sacred plant associated with Second Adar is the *lu'lav* לולב, an imma-
ture Palm Branch that hasn't opened yet. Lu'lav is about tempering the
extremes, constricting the expanses of Spirit Presence so that we are not
overwhelmed by Spirit Presence and lose our free will. According to the
teachings of the sixteenth-century Rabbi Yitzchak Luria of Safed, the tightly
constricted multi-layered foliage of the *lulav* is in itself a prayer tool intended
to constrict the Divine Light just enough so that it does not overwhelm
Creation.[56] Waving the *lu'lav*, then, is a shamanic ritual directed at invoking
balance in the Life Force by tempering the Light of Creation sufficiently to
enable individuation and life perpetuation, and to prevent the "black hole" of
the Creative Force from swallowing up Creation.

The act of waving this constricted "light beam" into the Four Directions,
Sky, Earth, and inward, addresses the seven sacred "pressure points" of the
te'heeru טהירו, the great primeval void into which the Infinite Source emanates its intention to manifest Creation. These seven pathways of Divine
Flow are Peace, Power, Wisdom, Life, Seed, Grace, and Bounty. These
seven attributes continuously weave their threads within Creation, directing
their gifts through "Infinite Depth of Upward, Infinite Depth of Downward,
Infinite Depth of East, Infinite Depth of West, Infinite Depth of North, Infinite Depth of South,"[57] and ultimately *Within*. "Within" is the Inner Sanctum
of every being, whether, stone, plant, animal or human. It is the heart of
hearts, the place of the Holy of Holies.[58] It is where the Primordial Thought
behind all existence becomes ensouled, becomes manifest; where it breathes
the Life Force into Creation.

Rabbi Luria's teaching goes on to describe the *sukkah* סוכה — the "lean-
to" we construct and eat in during the harvest season — as symbolic of the
womb of the feminine. The ceremony of waving the phallus-like *lu'lav* inside
the *sukkah* is then a rite of consummating the masculine energy of raw
intention with the feminine energy of transformation. It is a prayer that what
we seed into the soil at the doorway of Winter will impregnate the Earth for
birthing in Spring. This is likened to how the male impregnates the *sukkah*,
the womb, of the female with raw potential, with seed, after which the female
then brings it to fruition.

One of the intentions behind waving the *lu'lav* to the four winds, to the
sky, and to the Earth, is about warding off harsh winds and damaging weather.[59] This is why we do this ritual during our Harvest celebrations in Autumn,
which to us is the beginning phase of Winter. We wave the *lu'lav* then as a
ceremony of tempering extreme weather so that what we just seeded in

Summer and Fall is not damaged and is rather supported in growth and unfolding.

Lu'lav also represents shelter, and oasis. It is symbolic of hope in the wilderness of hopelessness; nurturance in the struggle with drought and famine, as the palm tree provided our ancestors with shade from the fiercely burning desert Sun; nourishment from its dates, fodder for our herds, and material for our baskets and other implements. And usually it meant water was nearby. It was also used to fan the sacred incense blend so that the fires on the rocks where the herbs were blended would burn continuously.

The House of Second Adar is: *bayt ha'ha'fah'chah* בית ההפכה, House of Upheaval, as in turning everything on its head. This is related to the study of Torah, or to figuring out a truth. One of the great sages of the first century, Ben Bahg-Bahg, insisted that to really get to the core of the teachings of the Torah, you have to turn it upside down and inside out until you get it. In Hebrew: *Hah'fahch bah ve'hah'fahch bah, deh koo'lah bah u'bah tech'zey*: הפך בה והפך בה דכולא בה ובה תחזי — "Turn her over and over, for everything is within her, and only through this will you truly see [meaning, only through that process will your perspective become clear]."[60]

Upheaval rouses fresh aliveness, brings forth the best or worst in us. It is about standing up to face the waves, and sometimes the Tsunami, of change in our lives, especially unanticipated shifts in the flow of our day-to-day life walk. But it is there, in the eye of those storms, that our core self is called to the forefront from its hiding place. This is the frolic of Leviathan, the great Sea Dragon shrugging, causing huge waves to wash ashore and shatter our illusions about things, our preconceived notions, our presumptions and assumptions. The House of Upheaval reminds us that what we take for granted as known and revealed is actually cloaked in deep mystery, and that everything is actually more than it seems.

Being an extra moon added to the twelve moons of the ancient wheel, Second Adar has no opposite, no Shadow Moon or Shadow House. It stands by itself, weaving in and out of the system, threading the wheel with its unpredictable strands of harmony and upheaval, waxing and waning like the Moon.

No wonder, then, that the Zodiac for this month is the North Star *ko'chav tza'fo'nah* כוכב צפונה, North being symbolic of Mystery, of Hiddenness, of *nees'tar* נסתר. And the letter of the Hebrew alphabet corresponding to this month is *alef* א , the first letter, symbolic of beginning, of Genesis, as upheaval brings renewal. Just like in the Creation story, where Creation emerges from out of the תהו, *to'hu*, the chaos. Interestingly, the word *to'hu* also translates as Wandering, Meandering. Like Deenah wandering about and dancing everyone into upheaval. Jacob now has to relocate because of her, after settling in too comfortably near Sh'chehm.[61]

The א is symbolic of the seeds of all beginnings. This is why the Creation story does not begin with this letter, but starts with the second letter of the alphabet, *bet* ב. The א is Mystery, hiddenness. It is actually a blend of three letters, two *yuds* י י — one above and one below — and a ו *wahv* running diagonally between them. Their numerical value, or *Gemmatria* גמטריא, is 26, the same Gemmatria as the Tetragrammaton, the *yud hay vahv hay*. י is 10, ה is 5, ו is 6, and the second ה is 5 — equalling 26. It is the same with the two *yuds* and the *wahv* in Alef. The י above is 10, the י below is another 10, and ו is 6 — equaling 26 as well. *Yud* is representative of the seed, the point of Genesis, the *nekudah sah'tee'mah* נקודה סתימה, the Concealed Point within which all emanates, all is born, and all possibility resides.[62] The י above is that core seed, so to speak, in the Spirit Realm, and the י below is that core seed planted within the Physical Realm, each representing, respectively, God transcendent and God immanent. The two realms are separated by the ו *wahv*, by the "And" which is what ו means. This "and" is the connecting *rah'kee'a* רקיע, usually translated as Firmament, the invisible, illusory divider or veil between the spirit world and the physical world. So the Alef is being referred to in the Torah narrative of the Creation story where it says: "And Elo'heem said, 'Let there be a *rah'kee'a,* a layer between the upper waters and the lower waters,'"[63] or: "Let there be a ו *wahv* between the upper י *yud* and the lower י *yud.*" Let there be an "And" connecting the two — let Creator and Creation always be accessible to one another. We are not the same, but we are one.

And so may it be, as we come full circle and open the windows of our hearts to the ever-renewing cycles of our journey, and with the ever-fresh wisdom of our most trusted traveling companion: Moon.

NOTES

1. Exodus 12:2 and 13:4.
2. Deuteronomy 28:12 and Ezekiel 34:26.
3. Isaiah 65:24.
4. Genesis 37:35.
5. *Midrash Tanchuma, Va'yey'shehv*, Ch. 10.
6. Genesis 34:1.
7. Genesis 30:20.
8. Genesis 30:21.
9. Genesis 30:21-22.
10. *Talmud Bav'li, Berachot* 60a and *Talmud Yerushalmi* 66b.
11. *Midrash Pirkei D'Rebbe Eliezer*, Ch. 35.
12. Genesis 34:25.
13. *Midrash B'reisheet Rabbah* 80:11.
14. *Midrash B'reisheet Rabbah* 19:12 and *Midrash Tanchuma, Vah'yeesh'lach*, Ch. 19.
15. *Talmud Bav'li, Sof'rim*, end of Ch. 21.
16. Genesis 41:45; *Midrash Pirkei D'Rebbe Eliezer*, Ch. 37. In Genesis 41:45 Ahsnaht is referred to as the daughter of Potifera; this is because Potifera had adopted her when she arrived in Egypt.

17. Genesis 34:3.
18. *Ohr HaChayyim ahl HaTorah, Breisheet*, 28:5 and 49:10.
19. *Talmud Bav'li, Avodah Zarah* 18a, *Berachot* 11a, *Eruvin* 53b, *Pesachim* 62b, and *Tosefta Kay'lim* 1:3; *Midrash Tehilim* 104:27.
20. 16th-century Rabbi Yeshayahu ben Avraham in *Sefer Ha'Sh'lah Ha'Kadosh, Asarah Ma'amarot, Ma'amar Sh'lee'shee U'Ma'amar R'vee'ee*, No. 33.
21. Genesis 34:3.
22. Genesis 34:8.
23. Genesis 34:19.
24. Zohar, Vol. 3, folio 16b.
25. 16th-century Rabbi Yeshayahu ben Avraham in *Sefer Ha'Sh'lah Ha'Kadosh, Sefer B'reisheet, Parashat Chayay Sarah, Torah Ohr*, Ch. 2.
26. *Midrash B'reisheet Rabbah* 100:11.
27. 13th-century Rabbi Moshe (Moses) ben Nachmon in *Ramban ahl HaTorah, B'reisheet* 34:12.
28. *Mishnah, Avot* 1:7.
29. *Midrash B'reisheet Rabbah* 80:11.
30. Psalms 104:26.
31. Maharal in *B'er Ha'Golah, Ha'B'er Har'vee'ee*, folios 69-71.
32. *Battay Midrashot*, Vol. 1: *Seder Rabbah D'Breisheet*, No. 17.
33. *Talmud Bav'li Baba Bat'ra* 74b.
34. Jeremiah 31:21.
35. Zohar, Vol. 3, folio 201b.
36. *Midrash Tehilim* 104:22.
37. Genesis 1:9.
38. *Midrash Sh'mo't Rabbah* 15:22.
39. *Midrash Pirkei D'Rebbe Eliezer*, Ch. 37.
40. *Talmud Bav'li, Baba Batra* 75a.
41. *Mishnah, Avot* 3:13.
42. *Midrash Pesik'ta D'Rav Kahana* 2:4.
43. *Midrash Alfa Beita D'Ben Sira, Keta* 78.
44. *Otzar HaMidrashim, Cho'nayn, Keta Gimmel*.
45. *Battay Midrashot*, Vol. 1: *Seder Rabbah D'Breisheet*, No. 17.
46. Exodus, Chapters 25 through 39.
47. Job 37:22.
48. Exodus 25:18 and 31.
49. *Midrash B'reisheet Rabbah* 16:2.
50. *Talmud Bav'li, Tosefta Yoma* 4:14.
51. Genesis 2:11.
52. Maharal in *Gevuro't Hashem*, Chapter 46, folio 178.
53. *Talmud Bav'li, Berachot* 60b.
54. Maharal in *Chee'doo'shay Ah'ga'do't, Kee'dusheen*, Vol. 2, folio 144.
55. Maharal in *Chee'doo'shay Ah'ga'do't, Sanhedrin*, Vol. 3, folio 241.
56. *Sefer Sha'ar Ha'Kavanot, Drashah* 3 and 5.
57. *Sefer Yetzirah* 1:6.
58. *Tikunei Zohar*, folio 137a.
59. *Talmud Bav'li, Menachot* 62a.
60. *Mishnah, Avot* 5:22.
61. Genesis 34:30 and 35:1.
62. Zohar, Vol. 1, folio 116b.
63. Genesis 1:6.

Index